A Garden of Love

Flowers from the Gethsemane Prayer Garden

Thomas B. Clarke

Bible Discernments
Publishing Division of Prayer Gardeners
Syracuse, NY USA

A Garden of Love
Copyright © 2009 by Thomas B. Clarke
Photographs by Thomas B. Clarke, Lukas Cluss, and Elaine Baker

Bible Discernments
Publishing Division of Prayer Gardeners
4113 W. Seneca Turnpike
Syracuse, NY 13215
www.Bible-Discernments.com

Printed in the United States of America

ISBN 978-0-9816213-2-6

All rights reserved. No part of this publication may be reproduced, stored in a retrieval system, or transmitted in any form or by any means – electronic, mechanical, photocopy, recording, or any other – except for brief quotations in printed reviews, without the permission of the author.

All Scripture quotations are taken from the *Holy Bible*, New Living Translation, Second Edition, copyright © 1996, 2004. Used by permission of Tyndale House Publishers, Inc., Wheaton, Illinois 60189. All rights reserved.

For a photographic review of the Gethsemane Prayer Garden, including what is in bloom each month, see www.PrayerGardeners.com/Gethsemane/

Contents

Gethsemane Prayer Garden
Introduction

Anemone	- 2 -
Astilbe	- 4 -
Autumn Joy	- 6 -
Bellflower	- 8 -
Blanket Flower	- 10 -
Bleeding Heart	- 12 -
Chrysanthemum	- 14 -
Columbine	- 16 -
Coneflower	- 18 -
Cosmos	- 20 -
Cranesbill	- 22 -
Daffodils	- 24 -
Delphinium	- 26 -
Flax and Soapwort	- 28 -
Forget-Me-Not	- 30 -
Gaura	- 32 -
Grape Hyacinth	- 34 -
Honeysuckle Vine	- 36 -
Hyssop	- 38 -
Iris	- 40 -
Jacob's Ladder	- 42 -
Lamb's Ear	- 44 -
Lavender	- 46 -
Lily	- 48 -
Marsh Marigold	- 50 -
Phlox	- 52 -
Primrose	- 54 -
Rose	- 56 -
Russian Sage	- 58 -
Showy Primrose	- 60 -

Index
About the Author

Dedication

To my Lord Jesus Christ –
 Lord, I love you. May you somehow use this book to touch the lives of others.

To my wife Nancy –
 On May 26, 1997, we took a trip to the beautiful Royal Botanical Gardens in Hamilton, Ontario along with another couple. The tulips were still out that day – like trays full of tea cups that were laid out for a Queen, we saw more color than the eye could behold. There were beds of red and white tulips, and then some orange and red ones. Some were white with frilly tops, others were tall and slender yellow-flowered. There were the fancy orange and green parakeet tulips and even some purple ones. Each flower bed was more abundant than the last – masses and masses of breath-taking color.

 I took your hand that day even though you had no understanding that I had my eyes on you. What you thought was an act of kindness was really setting a direction that would be for the rest of our lives. I found in you a kindred spirit, a lover of flowers, and a worshipper of Jesus Christ; we were married four months later.

 As with the Song of Solomon, we have entered the garden together. May we continue to increase in the love of Christ. I love and cherish you dearly.

 Three are even better, for a triple-braided cord is not easily broken (Ecclesiastes 4:12).

 Come, let us tell of the Lord's greatness; let us exalt his name together (Psalm 34:3).

Gethsemane Prayer Garden

The Gethsemane Prayer Garden at Faith Chapel was developed as a place for people to meet with the Lord. Faith Chapel is a non-denominational church located on Onondaga Hill in Syracuse, New York. The garden is open to Christians of all faiths.

Compared to other flower gardens that are open to the public, this garden is quite small. The garden began development in 2003 with two flower beds – as of the writing of this book in 2009, this one-acre site has expanded to now include nine beds (8,000 sq. ft.) with fifty perennial flower varieties and several hundred shrubs and trees from forty species and subspecies.

What makes this small garden unique is the strong emphasis on knowing the Lord's loving presence, hearing his voice, and responding to his love. Benches are available for a quiet time with the Lord. As we begin to experience the Lord's love for us, we find that an inner peace and gentleness often descends over us.

This garden is more than just a pretty place with lots of beautiful flowers. Rather, the flowers are intended to help soften our hearts so that we may be more effective in speaking to and hearing the voice of the Lord.

For those that decide to visit the garden, our hope is that you will see it as an outdoor sanctuary. In the garden, we hear our Lord speaking his loving words to us. Through the flowers and beauty of God's creation, our joy is to see hearts respond in love.

Some people have used the garden as a place of refuge during a difficult time – a parent, spouse, or even a child dies, sudden illness of someone we love, or the rebellion of a child. Whatever the difficulty, the Gethsemane Prayer Garden is a place where we can ask the Lord to help us and to seek answers to "Why?" While Faith Chapel can only provide Christian counseling to a very limited number of people, we believe that the Holy Spirit is our Counselor and he can provide that help.

Information about the church may be found at www.FaithChapelOnLine.org. A photographic preview of the garden, identifying what is in bloom from April through October, may be seen at www.PrayerGardeners.com/Gethsemane.

Parenthetical note: The congregation at Faith Chapel has limited financial means. As a medium-sized body of believers, many of whom are young adults, our goal is to reach out to our community and beyond about our Lord Jesus Christ. Please feel free to give us a visit if you are in the area. And, if you are especially touched by something in the garden or in this book, please consider a donation of any amount. Your gifts will be greatly appreciated and will help us enhance the prayer garden and spread this message of love.

Faith Chapel
4113 W. Seneca Turnpike (Rte 175)
Syracuse, NY 13152
www.FaithChapelOnLine.org

Acknowledgments

The Gethsemane Prayer Garden was first envisioned independently in 1999 by two people: Pastor Lee Simmons, founding pastor of Faith Chapel, and Alice Soule, a member of this church body. The garden was seen to be a quiet place of refuge and peace; a place similar to the garden in Jerusalem where Jesus offered his cup before the Lord in prayer; a place to have an encounter with the Lord.

Four years later, under the direction of Pastor Lee Simmons, the garden began development as a result of an initial bereavement gift. First, the gentle *'Bonica'* roses were added, followed in subsequent years with a stone altar, then several privacy berms, the addition of a trellis, and finally the relocation of a large number of shrubs and trees. As each area was developed and as finances permitted, perennials were brought in and walkways were added to create a cohesive and flowing effect.

Pastor Lee has been the Barnabas, the great encourager from the Book of Acts, in promoting the garden. He has been a living personification of Hebrews 10:24, *"Let us think of ways to motivate one another to acts of love and good works."* His continual support and positive words through the years have helped push this effort, allowing the garden to fulfill the vision from 1999.

While Tom Clarke has been the caretaker of the garden for most of those years, there have been sixty volunteers that have helped in one fashion or another in developing and maintaining this garden. Without the help of these volunteers, the garden would not be what it is today. The majority of volunteer hours have been given by teens who willingly devoted their time and effort while learning the skill of landscaping – a skill that they can use in financing their college education.

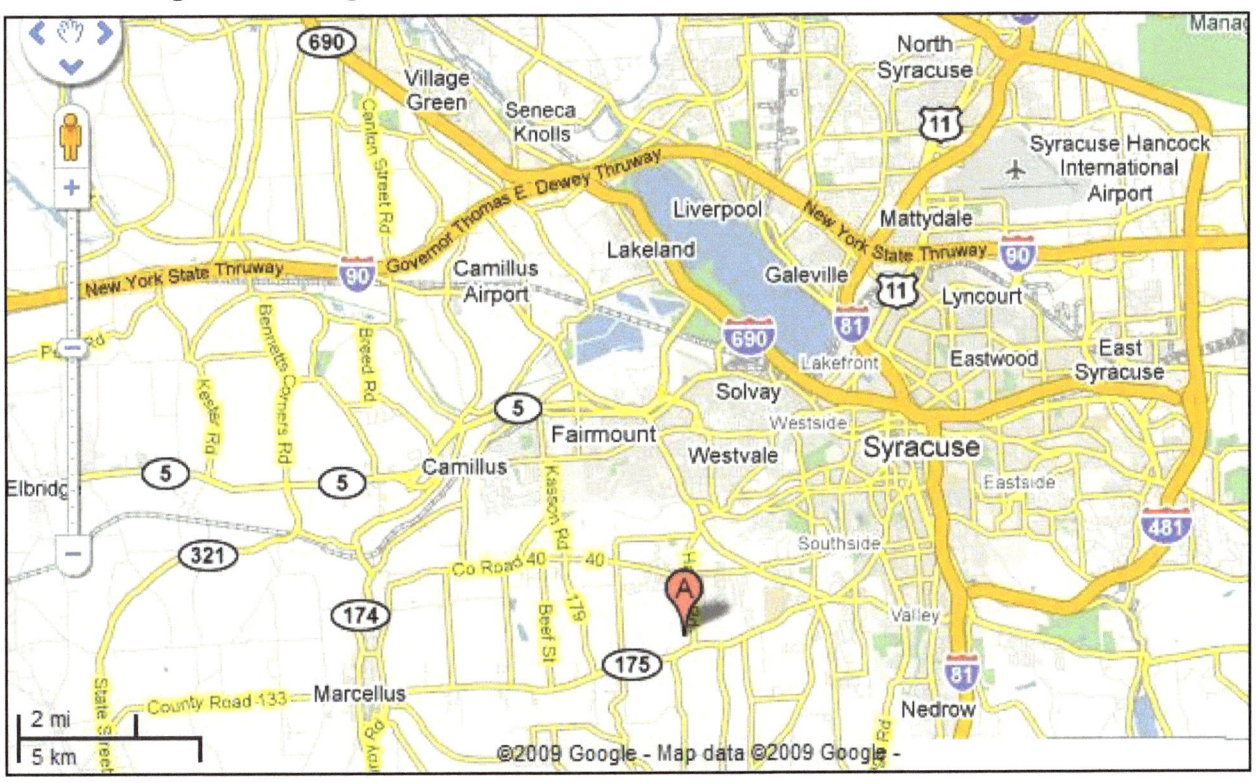

Introduction

> *"'You must love the LORD your God with all your heart, all your soul, and all your mind.' This is the first and greatest commandment. A second is equally important: 'Love your neighbor as yourself.' The entire law and all the demands of the prophets are based on these two commandments"* (Matthew 22:37-40).

Looking out from our retreat's mountaintop cabin, the valleys below are filled with the morning fog, like gentle, white pillows resting between the hills; the air is still as the new day unfolds. Slowly the scene changes as the sun warms the white blanket, alternately rising and falling. A new day is before us; another day to love.

A meadow of white and yellow wildflowers sits below the cabin. Clusters of black-eyed Susans dot the large field, only to be surrounded by a profusion of white Queen Anne's lace. Closer inspection reveals pink clover and purple asters that complement the spectrum. The grace and beauty of our Lord is revealed once again; his love for us is never ending.

As the air gets warmer on this September morning, the grasshoppers have started their late summer song, dragon flies have begun mating, and butterflies flit from place to place, from flower to flower, in a seemingly random flight to nowhere. Off in the distance, king birds fly from place to place searching for food, robins patiently listen for the movement of a worm, and Canada geese anxiously seek out their next cornfield. God's creation is teaching us how to love.

Do the plants and the animals know love, or is that reserved just for mankind? Can a pansy demonstrate love to another pansy? Does the earthworm know its Creator? Certainly the mother bear reveals her protective love over her cubs, but does that love extend to other female bears? More likely, these creatures are a special gift, showing us more of God's love.

In an orchestra, the violin soothes and the flute sings. In the nursery, the baby cries while the mother softly recalls a lullaby from her childhood. At night, the gentle breeze stirs against the leaves of the trees. Each sound is distinct to our ears, each showing its own purpose and place in this world that is God's creation – God's manifest love.

No single plant or animal, sound, smell, touch, or anything else can adequately describe God's love for us, or how our response should be. The Bible tells us to love our Lord, and then demonstrate this love through our thoughts, actions, and activities. Jesus said we are to love the Lord with everything that we have: our hearts, our souls, our minds, and our strength. His creation models the love he has for us. Can we love him in return with everything that we do, say, think, and every emotion of our being?

Jesus said that our love for our Lord and for one another is the greatest requirement for our lives. The various writers of the New Testament reiterated it and Christian writers from the earliest of times have emphasized this. Our response to our Lord's love for us is to be seen in everything we say and do – in our worship of our Lord and our treatment of one another. We as Christians are called to be effervescent – bubbling over with this kind of love.

Why another book on God's love? It is the power of the simile, where one idea is similar to another. Jesus often used similes such as when he spoke,

> *"A good tree can't produce bad fruit, and a bad tree can't produce good fruit. ... A good person produces good things from the treasury of a good heart, and an evil person produces evil things from the treasury of an evil heart"*
> (Luke 6:43,45).

Similes, like parables, offer an effective way of demonstrating abstract concepts – the symbolism can help us grasp the intent of the Scriptures in a more profound way.

This book identifies four different ways that deep heartfelt love appears in the Scriptures:
- Love of the Father to his Son
- Love of the Father, Son, and Holy Spirit to people
- Love of Christians to the Lord
- Love of Christians to one another

The first two of these we simply observe and receive – we are responsible for the last two areas of love.

The Lord wants to break down our hard-hearted walls that have been formed around us. Regarding our love back to the Godhead, this is identified by how much faith, trust, obedience, and zeal we have for our Lord. With respect to our love for others, this can be seen by our hearts of compassion, kindness, gentleness, humility, forgiveness, and grace as we daily interact with one another.

By interweaving a depiction of flowers and the Scriptures, this book attempts to illustrate how flowers can sometimes inspire a Scriptural application of love. Thirty flowering plants are presented – each photograph was taken in the Gethsemane Prayer Garden.

While this book is illustrated with many beautiful photographs, my hope is that the reader will take the meaning of each flower, apply it to the related teaching, and achieve a fresh understanding of Christian love. As a cello and violin duet can bring an inner calmness to our hearts, this photographic teaching on flowers is intended to help soften our hearts towards love. In this way, we demonstrate what is most important – *"faith expressing itself as love"* (Galatians 5:6).

I have been struck over the years by how the Holy Spirit has shown me a Scriptural understanding of a flower, shrub, or tree. In writing this book, that deeper understanding was greatly accelerated. Each flower's teaching reveals different aspects of Christian love; this book records how the Holy Spirit spoke to me about becoming a more loving Christian. Rather than being an authority on either gardening or on love, this book records how the Holy Spirit instructed me about love and how he used flowers to accomplish that purpose.

Your discernment about a particular flower may be different than mine and that is perfectly fine. My hope is that you will personally experience the love of our Lord Jesus Christ through these photographs and devotions.

While I am not able to personally respond to all eMail, I greatly appreciate your correspondence. You may contact me at PrayerGardeners@hotmail.com.

Thomas B. Clarke
Caretaker, Gethsemane Prayer Garden

Above all, clothe yourselves with love, which binds us all together in perfect harmony
(Colossians 3:14).

Anyone who does not love does not know God, for God is love
(1 John 4:8).

A Garden of Love

Anemone

One of my most favorite flowers is the Japanese anemone with its soft pinkish-lavender hues, so bountifully presented. And oh, the many, many honey bees this flower attracts, filling our ears with the sound of their activity! With this plant, I invite you to experience the depth of God's love.

Depth of the Love of Christ

The Japanese anemone presents an abundant wealth of softly hued pinkish-lavender blossoms. In July, many tight blossoms first appear on open stems above the dark green leaves; by August, some of these elegant blossoms have opened while others wait until September or October, resulting in three months of profuse flowering. During this time, countless numbers of honey bees enthusiastically flit from blossom to blossom, seeking to be filled with the anemone's nectar. The flowers have no discernible fragrance, yet its food is God-given life and power for the bees.

Just as the nectar from the anemone fills the bee, Paul wrote of fullness in his letter to the Ephesians:

> *Then you will be made complete with all the fullness of life and power that comes from God (Ephesians 3:19).*

That fullness is the divine presence of God, manifested as a flood of God's Holy Spirit.

How do we receive this fullness? Paul explained in that same verse: *"May you experience the love of Christ … [so that] … you will made complete with all the fullness of life and power"* (Ephesians 3:19). To the honey bee, it experiences this fullness from the nectar. To the Christian, we experience it through Christ's love.

> *I pray that from his glorious, unlimited resources he will empower you with inner strength through his Spirit. Then Christ will make his home in your hearts as you trust in him. Your roots will grow down into God's love and keep you strong. And may you have the power to understand, as all God's people should, how wide, how long, how high, and how **deep** his love is. May you experience the love of Christ, though it is too great to understand fully. Then you will be made complete with all the fullness of life and power that comes from God (Ephesians 3:16-19).*

Lord, help us to understand how wide, how long, how high, and how deep your love is. We can think of width, from side to side; of length, from front to back; and height, from top to bottom. Depth, on the other hand, is not a dimension in the same way – it allows us to look beyond the geometry, into the unique and endless attributes of God's creation.

The Japanese anemone shows depth in its soft colors of pink to lavender; in its sweet nectar for the honey bees; in its fresh dew in the evening; and in its persistence to keep on growing. The roots of the anemone are among the hardest to remove from a planted area because the roots are so persistent. This, too, is part of depth.

The depth of God's love has endless applications: to a bird, depth is experienced in various wind speeds; to a farmer, the smells of spring are different from those of autumn; to a life guard, the blue sky of morning is different at mid-day; to a skier, the snow on a warm day is different than when it is frigid; to an owl, the light at night is preferred over the brightness of day. Wherever we go, whatever we do, God's love is evident.

Paul's prayer for fellow believers in Ephesians 3:16-19 is hope that we might experience the depth of the love of Christ, dwelling richly with him in glory. In this way, we become like the anemone, a representation of deep, true love.

Astilbe

I so appreciate the softness and serenity that is associated with the astilbe. The plumes can be creamy white, burnt red, or soft pink, each one appearing as soft as cotton candy. As we approach the area of the cooler shaded astilbe, see if you can feel the invitation — "Come, enjoy, rest here for a while."

Humility and Gentleness

Plumes of creamy white, burnt red, royal purple, peachy coral, and soft pink, each as soft as cotton candy, reach out from its shaded location inviting the garden visitor, "Can you gently touch me?" Blooming for four weeks in mid-summer, the vigorous astilbe flowers refresh us like a soft breeze that comes into the valley on a summer evening. The plume effect is created by a clustering of tiny flowers, delicately and gracefully gathered around a central stalk.

The gentle softness of the astilbe is reminiscent of the immense peace that we can sometimes experience in the presence of the Lord. As limp as a dish rag and consumed by an overwhelming sense of peace and quietness, at those moments, nothing is greater than our Lord – our own needs are lost; our Lord is everything and all consuming. Here, the softness and gentleness of our Lord envelops us; peace encapsulates us; love surrounds us. If only it would last forever.

Help us, dear Lord, to enter into that place, to be deeply in your presence. Take us away from ourselves. Amen.

Some people say that they are too overwhelmed with life to enjoy his presence. Jesus calls to those who are weary; to those who are burdened with too much of today's troubles; to those who are too busy with life. He says *"I will give you rest ... rest for your souls"* (Matthew 11:28,29). Do you want freedom from being overwhelmed with today? Jesus says that he will provide that rest. But how?

> *"Come to me, all of you who are weary and carry heavy burdens, and I will give you rest. Take my yoke upon you. Let me teach you, because I am humble and gentle at heart, and you will find rest for your souls. For my yoke is easy to bear, and the burden I give you is light"* (Matthew 11:28-30).

Jesus wants to replace your weariness, troubles, and busyness with a new yoke and a new burden. It is really not a yoke at all, but it is softness and gentleness. In this way, your reaction to your cares is replaced with humility and gentleness. This is the Lord's presence within us.

Buried in the middle of these verses is Jesus' softhearted and satisfying answer to the weary: *"Let me teach you, because I am humble and gentle at heart"* (Matthew 11:29). Jesus is saying that as we enter his rest, allow him to help us become like the astilbe, soft and gentle. No matter how weary, burdened, or busy we are, no matter what obstacles we have in front of us, his rest teaches us how to become humble and yielding like Christ. Paraphrasing, Jesus says *"Allow me to teach you my softness, my humility; become like me in humbleness and gentleness as you receive my rest; in this way, you will overcome your weariness and heavy burdens."*

Help us, dear Lord, to enter that rest; to be in your presence; to help us deal with our situations. Teach us your humility and grace. Amen.

A Garden of Love

Autumn Joy

During the heat of the summer months, I sometimes wonder if the autumn joy will be ready for their fall display. And then, moments later it seems, their joyful pinkish-red flowers burst forth. These aptly-named flowers gently remind me how Jesus said that in order to have complete joy, we are to love others as he loves each of us.

Joy in Loving

September is a month of change – the tree leaves begin their awesome transformation from green to their autumn yellow, orange, red, and even purple colors; nuts fall to the ground, much to the glee of scampering squirrels; many birds begin their long migration paths from north to south, sometimes in mass and sometimes alone; and wooly caterpillars inch along in hope of reaching a better place before the onset of cold winds.

The garden is in transition during September as well – the purple coneflowers have faded in color, the cranesbill have long stopped flowering, and the columbine have started their new growth for the next spring. Yet several plants show their beauty during September, and the autumn joy with its broccoli-shaped flowers is one of these splendid plants. Patiently, these flowers have waited to open, first as a blush of pink that soon transitions to various shades of red or purple, and then to deeper magenta by mid to late fall.

By contrast, the autumn joy pales in comparison to the rejoicing that we experience when we love as Christ loves.

> *"I have loved you even as the Father has loved me. Remain in my love. … I have told you these things so that you will be filled with my joy. Yes, your joy will overflow! This is my commandment: Love each other in the same way I have loved you. There is no greater love than to lay down one's life for one's friends"* (John 15:9,11-13).

Notice the words, *"… you will be filled with my joy"* and *"your joy will overflow!"*

Sammy was a little three-year-old boy who, along with the rest of his class, was taken on an outing by his Sunday School teacher. She had prepared her class about caring for others, and had shown them photographs of elderly people who sat around a nursing home all day. She knew about the elderly in this home because her mother was one of them. Her mother, in her time, was one of the most loving Sunday School teachers, and now her daughter was following in her footsteps.

On the day of the field trip, Sammy had taken a brief trip to his back yard with a small plastic bag from the store. Finding his prize, he stuck it in his pocket for safe keeping. Soon the class of twelve was off to the nursing home with their mothers and the teacher. Sammy was the only one to bring a present. When they got to the room of the teacher's mother, he joyously presented her with a big brown toad.

Grace prevailed. The elderly woman, with a big smile on her face, instructed her daughter to dump out a fragrant bouquet of white roses that had been recently delivered. Into the clear glass vase went the toad along with a few leaves from the bouquet, topped with a heavy book to keep the nursing staff happy. Her thank you was genuine, for she knew how to love. And Sammy was learning the same.

As the autumn joy is a beautiful, joyous plant to our eyes, so we become a joy when Christ's love overflows from us. Emanating from our deep relationship with Christ is the filling and overflowing of joy that results from truly loving.

A Garden of Love

Bellflower

A soft, contented smile comes over my face as I gaze at the bell-shaped bellflower blossoms. Adorned in their royal purple colors, I can almost imagine how these small bells would sound, ringing softly and gently as they proclaim their good news: the Lord is head over heals in love with us, and he is eagerly waiting for our loving response.

Love – the Highest Goal

The bellflower (or *Campanula* if you prefer) is an enamoring border or rock garden plant that offers an intriguing number of forms and shapes. The deep-purple flower shown on the opposite page is the *'Sarastro'* bellflower, a recent hybrid that appears to softly ring a delicate tone of loving affection. Each bellflower seems to have its own melodious ring.

In the Berkshire Mountains of western Massachusetts, the Boston Symphony conducts their summer evening concerts on the lawn at Tanglewood. The dew begins to fall as the concert begins – soon, the sun has set leaving just the lighting from the orchestra and walkway areas. One by one, children fall asleep on their blankets or in their mother's arms as the concert proceeds to their final piece by Tchaikovsky. Softly the orchestra plays as if in a dream of angels on wings – everything is peaceful and harmonious, absolutely lovely. The ambiance is unforgettable. Suddenly, a cannon shoots a bloodthirsty boom from the center of the audience, the concluding portion of the *1812 Overture*. Children are crying and everyone is in shock – the peace is gone. Cannons don't belong in the orchestra.

> *Love is patient and kind. Love is not jealous or boastful or proud or rude. It does not demand its own way. It is not irritable, and it keeps no record of being wronged. It does not rejoice about injustice but rejoices whenever the truth wins out. Love never gives up, never loses faith, is always hopeful, and endures through every circumstance ... Love will last forever!*
> (1 Corinthians 13:4-8).

The bellflower, with graceful blossoms that arch over one another in humility, is a simple example of how patient, kind, continuous, hopeful, and enduring our love should be. In a non-assuming way, they seem to gently ring their melody in unison – a song that is not noisy or like a clanging cymbal: *"If I could speak all the languages of earth and of angels, but didn't love others, I would only be a noisy gong or a clanging cymbal"* (1 Corinthians 13:1).

Lack of love disrupts; the presence of deep and profound love unifies and brings us closer to our Lord who is ready to send whatever physical or spiritual blessings he may have for us.

This section of the Scriptures concludes with this:

> *Three things will last forever – faith, hope, and love – and the greatest of these is love. Let love be your highest goal! (1 Corinthians 13:13;14:1).*

These verses emphasize the importance of love being manifested throughout our lives. Whatever our regrets in life, our Lord is looking at how we love today, not dwelling on the irritable things we may have done in the past. God is looking for changed hearts – hearts that truly love.

The softly ringing bellflower seems to understand that love is its highest goal.

Blanket Flower

When I glance at the red and yellow blanket flower, I see each flower head displaying itself like a small lamp – a beacon of light. I like to plant masses of these simple but adoring flowers together as a statement of vibrant life and contentedness. These flowers represent to me a group of loving Christian believers, for Jesus said he is the light unto the world so that we may become his children of light.

Children of the Light

The blanket flower has cheery, happy blossoms that smile back seemingly saying "I am a child of the light." Some varieties have deep red petals, as those shown on the opposite page – more commonly the deep red petals have a yellow fringe on the tip of each petal. Also known by their Latin name *Gaillardia*, these daisy-shaped flowers offer a simplicity that is found in few other flowers of its size.

The key to having a regular and continuous succession of flower blooms on the blanket flower is to periodically cut off the older blossoms. Each of the blood-red flowers, after six to ten days in the sunlight, will drop their petals only to reveal a red, sun-shaped seed head that quickly turns to a muted yellow. This seed head, as shown above, has the appearance of a small round light bulb or a miniature image of the sun – in time, this light bulb will dry up and turn grayish-brown as the seeds mature.

In the Bible, Jesus said *"I am the light of the world. If you follow me, you won't have to walk in darkness, because you will have the light that leads to life"* (John 8:12). What does he mean when he says to *"follow me"*? Consider these words from Ephesians:

> *Imitate God, therefore, in everything you do, because you are his dear children. Live a life filled with love, following the example of Christ. He loved us and offered himself as a sacrifice for us, a pleasing aroma to God. ... Don't be fooled by those who try to excuse ... sins, for the anger of God will fall on all who disobey him. Don't participate in the things these people do. For once you were full of darkness, but now you have light from the Lord. So live as people of light!* (Ephesians 5:1,2,6-8).

Where this translation uses the words *"people of light"* in the last verse, most translators follow a more literal reading from the Greek: *"children of light."* The conclusion is readily apparent: Jesus is the light; following that light leads to life; to follow that life, we are to be filled with love; by imitating his love, we live as children of the light (who is Jesus).

Next time you come across the blanket flower, consider speaking back to it, saying "I too am a child of the light, for I truly love from the depth of my heart."

A Garden of Love

Bleeding Heart

I, like many others, see the soft, pink heart-shaped blossoms on the bleeding heart as representing a sense of passion or compassion for others. Those people that are most sensitive and caring, delicate and enamoring, listening and attentive – those are the ones I see represented by the bleeding heart. Jesus is the ultimate example of this, as he calls us to be tenderhearted and sympathetic towards one another.

Compassion

The old-fashioned bleeding heart has been fancied in gardens for years with its many heart-shaped flowers, often as a symbol of a compassionate heart. Long sprays of soft pink, red, or white flowers arch over fern-like leaves, providing a wealth of blossoms for several weeks in the mid-spring. To some, the bleeding heart is also a symbol of love.

After these sensitive little flowers have finished blossoming, the leaves turn yellow and sometimes shrivel away – soon, the plant is in dormancy until the following spring. Regarding love, the apostle Paul wrote, *"Love never gives up, never loses faith, is always hopeful, and endures through every circumstance"* (1 Corinthians 13:7). What is a gardener to do, when the plant that best typifies a sensitive heart fades away? Plant Japanese anemone.

A technique sometimes called "succession planting" can be used to take care of these bare spots – in this way, flowers with different bloom periods are planted in the same vicinity, one almost on top of the other. At the top right of the photo on the opposite page, Japanese anemone can be seen at just a few inches tall. Ultimately the Japanese anemone will tower over the area and the once beautiful bleeding heart will be nowhere to be found. In this way, succession planting allows a late developing perennial to be planted in the same vicinity as a plant that matures in the spring. Similarly, this technique is also used to intersperse daffodils with Russian sage, hiding the leggy daffodil leaves as they mature.

Regarding a compassionate, bleeding heart, Paul wrote these instructions to Peter,

> *All of you should be of one mind. Sympathize with each other. Love each other as brothers and sisters. Be tenderhearted, and keep a humble attitude* (1 Peter 3:8).

Mary Magdalene is one such person that typifies a compassionate heart. She had personally witnessed the crucifixion of Jesus Christ, so she knew he had died and had been placed in the tomb. But we do know that on the morning after the Sabbath, she was the first person there. Imagine her fear, her frustration, even her anguish as she anxiously told Peter and John, *"'They have taken the Lord's body out of the tomb, and we don't know where they have put him!'"* (John 20:2).

Peter and John rushed to the scene and came to a new understanding about Christ, yet no heartfelt emotion is recorded. On the other hand, look at Mary – she was still crying and weeping. Through her tears, she pleaded similar words to the next visitors at the scene because Peter and John had not resolved her heartache. She said to the angels, *"'They have taken away my Lord ... and I don't know where they have put him'"* (John 20:13).

Mary Magdalene was a person who had sincere compassion for others. That is what the bleeding heart reminds us – tenderhearted and sympathetic love for one another.

A Garden of Love

Chrysanthemum

In the chrysanthemum, I see hope and restoration, a promise of good things to come, and an abundance of blessings. Visitors to hospitals and homes for the elderly often lovingly present a "mum" to the patient, sending a message of encouragement with its many rich autumn colors, their prolific blooms and their cheery presence. In a similar way, Jesus offered hope near the time of his death, stating, *"I will see you again; then you will rejoice, and no one can rob you of that joy"* (John 16:22).

Reconciliation

In the late summer, as the sun gets lower and the evenings become longer, large attractive displays of chrysanthemums begin appearing at garden stores, hardware stores, grocery stores, and large retail stores. The appeal of having strong autumnal colors seems irresistible to many. Everybody seems to get into the act, desiring to overcome the fading colors of summer with a fall color pick-me-up. Some enthusiasts are content to leave them in pots to brighten the front entrance to their home, while others happily plant them in the perfect corner or accent place in their garden. And some potted chrysanthemums are given as gifts – the following is a story about one such gift.

It had been six years since Billy and Marge had their final blowout. He had recently been laid off from his job in aeronautical engineering where he had been a research analyst, having received his Ph.D. from a university ten years earlier. Marge worked as a teacher, preferring that over staying at home with their two daughters.

Marge had become very frustrated with Billy's unstable and explosive manner, his long and exhausting hours at work, and his self-centered attitude. She would attempt to arrange family events where the four could be together, but they were always thwarted for one reason or another. Her friends, thinking they were offering wise advice, asked if she considered separation, but she always replied "No, at least not now."

Billy felt the weight of his wife's constant criticism; he knew she was pulling away from him. They often fought, ending in slammed doors where Billy returned to work for solace. Sometimes he slept there on the couch. That is until he lost his job.

The events on the night of their separation happened quickly. She said something, he got upset, she raised her voice, he slammed the door and she yelled "Don't come back!" With no job to return to, he started driving – in two days he was in another city with a broken down car, no job, no family, and no house to live in. He called his wife who told him she wanted to remain separated. Billy felt complete and total rejection.

Billy became a homeless man, living on the streets near the university, unkempt, unclean, and depressed. His day-to-day existence was to beg and live off of left-over food. His only contact with his family was at Christmas when he sent a card with a photo of himself.

Billy had been brought up in a Christian home; he and Marge had sporadically attended church services. A young man from a campus ministry gave Billy a Bible. Soon he started attending Sunday night services. In time, Billy shaved his face, got clean clothes and eventually became a teacher's aide at a Christian school. One day, Billy read in his Bible:

> *"So if you are presenting a sacrifice at the altar in the Temple and you suddenly remember that someone has something against you, leave your sacrifice there at the altar. Go and be reconciled to that person"* (Matthew 5:23,24).

Somehow these verses touched Billy's heart. He called Marge; to his amazement, they had a long conversation and she asked if he would like to come for a visit. There was no hesitation in Billy's voice, yet inwardly his memories of rejection brought both fear and joy to his mind. Two days later, on a September afternoon, Billy rang the doorbell of the same house he had lived in. Fumbling and crying, he offered three purplish red chrysanthemums, one for Marge and one for each daughter. Awestruck at the sight of a new man, Marge wept with joy.

Happily, they eventually became reunited, for Christ had helped her during the six years to come in touch with the secret desires of her heart.

A Garden of Love

Columbine

Strolling along through the mid-spring garden, I enjoy the delicate form and gentle sweetness in the old-fashioned columbine, sensing its grace and kindness. This variety is deep purple, not loud or boisterous, but a mellow, easily coordinated color that allows other flowers to shine. In this plant, I sense Jesus calling us Christians to show love and mercy to others through acts of kindness.

Kindness

The delicate columbine mixes shades of yellow, white, red, pink, purple, and blue to create seemingly infinite and often stunning combinations. With two sets of petals, the five rounded center petals are surrounded by an additional five pointed petals which often creates a two-toned effect. The flowers shown on the opposite page have the same rich purple color on the inner and outer petals, yet the star-shaped effect is the same.

Columbine are exceptionally easy to grow in well-drained locations in either full sun or partial shade. Patience may be required if planted from seed as they possibly may not bloom for two or more years – however, the wait is well worth it. Perfectly formed green scalloped leaves appear in the first year, followed by the exceptional color and delicacy in subsequent years.

Rather than picking out the best selection from a seed catalog, consider obtaining the seeds from a friend or neighbor, calling upon their goodness to share some of their bounty. Most homeowners enjoy the thrill of sharing their plant wealth, responding to the kind and admiring words spoken over their gardening efforts. However, if columbine is already blooming in your garden, introduction of another variety may cause hybridization.

One way to plant them is to scatter a mass of the seeds in a well-drained and lightly shaded bed shortly after the seeds start rattling in early summer. A two-foot by four-foot bed should ultimately produce fifty or more plants. Gently scratch the tiny seeds into the soil and lightly mulch – occasionally water if the soil becomes dry and remove weeds as necessary. New plants should be sprouted by the fall – leave them in this bed for another year, occasionally thinning and watering as necessary. Transplant them to the desired location the next spring – they should abundantly bloom roughly two or three years after the first sowing.

Paul wrote about sowing and reaping in his letter to the Galatians:

> *Don't be misled – you cannot mock the justice of God. You will always harvest what you plant. Those who live only to satisfy their own sinful nature will harvest decay and death from that sinful nature. But those who live to please the Spirit will harvest everlasting life from the Spirit. So let's not get tired of doing what is good. At just the right time we will reap a harvest of blessing if we don't give up. Therefore, whenever we have the opportunity, we should do good to everyone – especially to those in the family of faith* (Galatians 6:7- 10).

These verses describe how sowing good to others will reap a rich harvest. The investment of time, thoughts, and prayers will yield those blessings.

In his discussion about loving your enemies in the Sermon on the Mount, Jesus stated:

> *"If you love only those who love you, what reward is there for that? Even corrupt tax collectors do that much. If you are kind only to your friends, how are you different from anyone else? Even pagans do that"* (Matthew 5:46,47).

Therefore, kindness is not intended just for your friends and neighbors but for everyone. If you follow the above suggestion to have a friend or neighbor share some columbine seeds, a second opportunity for kindness appears when your blossoms finally open.

A Garden of Love

Coneflower

One of my thrills is coming to a fresh vision of a flower – recently that happened with the purple coneflower. As my eye drifted in its direction, I became aware of how much this flower resembled a crown, just as a king would wear. The bronze-brown center "eye" in the middle is surrounded by purple "rays", reminding me that one day, God's children will each wear a crown of righteousness.

Patient Endurance

The crowned glory of the mid-summer garden is the purple coneflower, abundantly proclaiming itself with simple daisy-shaped pink and purple flowers. The disk, which is the spiny bronze-brown "eye" at the center, appears insignificant when compared to the brightly colored rays, which are the purple whorls that radiate out from the center like a child's toy windmill. As the disk or "eye" hardens, the effect is a head surrounded by petals in a crown shape, similar to a crown that might be placed on a worthy king.

Like the crown of the purple coneflower, the Scriptures encourage us to pursue a "crown of righteousness" that will last for all of eternity:

> *And now the prize awaits me — the crown of righteousness, which the Lord, the righteous Judge, will give me on that great day of his return. And the prize is not just for me but for all who eagerly look forward to his glorious return* (2 Timothy 4:8).

The Apostle Paul was near the time of his death when he wrote this letter to his beloved spiritual son Timothy. He stated in the preceding verse that *"I have fought a good fight, I have finished the race, and I have remained faithful"* (2 Timothy 4:7). The goal for all Christians is to be able to state that they fought hard for the Christian cause and have remained faithful to it. For that, Paul was confident that he would receive that "crown of righteousness."

What will heaven be like? Like the purple coneflower, will there be clusters of people wearing their crown of righteousness? Will it be a literal crown that everyone can see, or will it be fixed in our spirits that only the Lord can see. We can only suppose.

Paul's ministry affected an untold multitude of people – even to this day, believers are profoundly changed as a result of his many messages, declared by a man that was passionate about the life-altering love of Jesus. In describing his own life, Paul stated why he believed he would receive that crown of righteousness: *"You know my faith, my patience, my love, and my endurance. You know how much persecution and suffering I have endured"* (2 Timothy 3:10,11). Note this – it was Paul's love that allowed him to endure all his suffering and hardships.

Paul wrote this letter from a prison in Rome after many long and difficult years of suffering – he had been imprisoned, whipped, beaten, and shipwrecked many times, faced death, and all kinds of dangers – yet he did not complain; he only loved.

> *So I am willing to endure anything if it will bring salvation and eternal glory in Christ Jesus to those God has chosen* (2 Timothy 2:10).

Paul endured all of these hardships because he loved. Just as *"God so loved the world ..."*, Paul too showed his love by giving his own life. Sincere love for one another is the true reason why Paul was worthy of receiving the crown of righteousness.

When we look at the purple coneflower, we might wonder if this is a picture of heaven – many heads that have received their crowns because of their sacrificial and patiently enduring love for one another.

A Garden of Love

Cosmos

If I could, I think I would plant acres of cosmos. Their flowers are so tall and wispy with an abundance of white, pink, and rose color that splash the color palette. As the flowers dance in the wind, I know that it is the strong roots that allow it to withstand heavy winds and storms. In this next reading, I invite you to see how else the cosmos withstand the storms.

Love Your Enemies

The many soft and delicate flowers of the cosmos, standing tall and wispy, seem to dance with each breath of wind. The leaves are almost hair thin and become unnoticeable in comparison to the flowers. Somehow, the combination of pinks and whites and soft reds, each with a center spot of bright yellow, leads to thoughts of compassion, gentleness, and grace.

One of the joys of these flowers is watching the yellow goldfinch land on the flower stems, looking for a good seedy meal. The weight of these tiny birds is just light enough to allow them to eat what they want and spill the extra flower seeds on the ground. In this way, next year's plants are sown for another season of color.

The roots of the cosmos spread very wide, enabling this tall plant to withstand strong forces of wind. The gusts come and the cosmos sways left and right with each new glance – the stabilizing roots hold onto the plant and return it to its upright position.

In life, we receive gusts of wind from people that have their own agendas. Nasty words are spoken, harshness is perceived and received, and harmful actions take place. How do we react to these acts of unkindness; how wide and deep are our roots?

Sometimes the wind gusts are so strong on the cosmos that parts of the plant are broken, usually at the weak spot where the branch meets the vertical stalk. The branch will bend towards the ground, revealing its hurt and pain. The broken branches are not hidden, for their hurts are exposed for all to see. In time, however, the flowers on that broken branch will reach out towards the sky, once again showing their beauty.

When the heavy rain comes, the flower heads turn towards the ground, bent over by the weight of the water. During these times, no longer does the flower reach towards the sky, but instead it yields under the heaviness. The graceful flowers protect themselves with humility.

How do we react to adversity? When people hurt us, curse us, or are unreasonably demanding, can our attitude be like the cosmos? Jesus said, *"Love your enemies! Do good to those who hate you"* (Luke 6:27).

He continues,

> *"Love your enemies! Do good to them. Lend to them without expecting to be repaid. Then your reward from heaven will be very great, and you will truly be acting as children of the Most High, for he is kind to those who are unthankful and wicked. You must be compassionate, just as your Father is compassionate"* (Luke 6:35,36).

The attitude revealed by the cosmos is being flexible when the winds blow, showing our hurts and pains when we are broken, and offering humility during the heavy rain. When we are kind and full of grace to difficult people, allowing the love of God that is within us to be revealed, then we are able to show the grace that Jesus describes.

A Garden of Love

Cranesbill

Look at how abundantly the cranesbill blossoms! These bright bluish-purple or bluish-pink flowers speak to me of the intense love that we are to express. The fullness of the cranesbill shows the zeal that we are to have in Christ: zealous for the Lord, full of his Spirit, and full of his love.

Love Deeply

Multitudes of two-inch pink, blue, purple, or white cup-shaped flowers provide a long season of full color. The cranesbill, also known as hardy geranium, opens in early summer and blooms for more than two months. When grown two or three feet apart and given a taste of fertilizer, the plants become so full of blossoms that one plant cannot be easily distinguished from another. The effect is a large mass of beautiful, exhilarating color.

Being full of blossoms may remind us of the term *"fullness of Christ"* (Ephesians 4:13) which is used to describe one who has developed spiritual maturity. Consider how the following verses, written by Paul to the church in Rome, represent this fullness of Christ:

> *Don't just pretend to love others. Really love them. Hate what is wrong. Hold tightly to what is good. Love each other with genuine affection, and take delight in honoring each other. Never be lazy, but work hard and serve the Lord enthusiastically. Rejoice in our confident hope. Be patient in trouble, and keep on praying. When God's people are in need, be ready to help them. Always be eager to practice hospitality.*
>
> *Bless those who persecute you. Don't curse them; pray that God will bless them. Be happy with those who are happy, and weep with those who weep. Live in harmony with each other. Don't be too proud to enjoy the company of ordinary people. And don't think you know it all!*
>
> *Never pay back evil with more evil. Do things in such a way that everyone can see you are honorable. Do all that you can to live in peace with everyone. Dear friends, never take revenge. Leave that to the righteous anger of God* (Romans 12:9-19).

Those who are full in Christ exhibit true, deep and sincere love for one other. God created every person to love and be loved – even the most difficult of people. He calls us to be genuine in affection and honor, hard-working, enthusiastic, joyous, patient, prayerful, compassionate, humble, and peace-seeking. This fullness is both genuine and sincere.

As the cranesbill's delicate flowers bloom, little attention is given to the plant's lovely leaves. Yet by autumn after the dead flower heads are removed, the deeply serrated leaves take on red, orange, and burgundy tones that brighten up the fall garden. This, too, adds to the fullness of the cranesbill.

In the example of the cranesbill, the fullness of the plant is promoted through the use of fertilizer. Even for a spiritually mature individual, the fertilizer is the love, encouragement, empathy, and harmony that we receive from others. We each have our part in this scenario. Love deeply.

Daffodils

Call me crazy, but I'm not much of an enthusiast of yellow in the garden, except in the spring. Yet to me, the bright yellow daffodils, sometimes white and occasionally with a tinge of pink, are a most gracious welcome after a long winter. The daffodils seem to proclaim what Jesus offers – the old life is gone and a new life has begun; a new person in Christ.

The New Journey with Christ

A bed of robust yellow stars, six-pointed and full of vigor, cheerfully greets the new spring day. Boldly the daffodils bring a new message of hope, proclaiming the good news that the death of winter is finally past. The oppressive winter winds, bitterly cold nights, freezing rain, and driving snow all seem behind. Even the pristine white days after a freshly fallen snow, sparkling in sun – even those days seem a burden when compared to the refreshingly warm days of spring. The simple and joyous message of the daffodil is "a new beginning."

The new spring that is presented by the daffodils is somehow similar to the new life we have in Jesus. We remember the winter for it has been such a part of our lives. At times we make winter out to be better than it was, especially on those colder days of spring when the rain comes and everything seems damp and dreary. But the cold and rainy days of spring are still necessary for feeding the roots and growing the plants as many new flowers begin to surface. The new life in Christ means we have overcome winter.

Besides the daffodils, there are many small and seemingly insignificant perennials that begin to sprout from the ground in the spring, offering only a tiny hint of their coming beauty. Often we hardly pay attention to these newly formed plants, not concentrating on their unique beauty. Instead of looking ahead, we tend to focus on the flowers that are currently in bloom and recall those from the immediate past.

Regarding what has past and what we see today, Paul wrote this to the Ephesians to throw that aside:

> *Since you have heard about Jesus and have learned the truth that comes from him, throw off your old sinful nature and your former way of life, which is corrupted by lust and deception. Instead, let the Spirit renew your thoughts and attitudes. Put on your new nature, created to be like God – truly righteous and holy* (Ephesians 4:21-24).

For the person that has begun their spiritual journey with Christ, let this be an encouragement so that we don't turn back. *"Do not bring sorrow to God's Holy Spirit by the way you live. Remember, he has identified you as his own. ... Live a life filled with love"* (Ephesians 4:30;5:2).

The daffodils represent that new beginning that Christ has taken us to, not turning back, but marching forward with the love and confidence of Jesus Christ who is living within us.

Delphinium

The tall delphinium, dressed in white, purple, blue, and even pink shades, is a beautiful and stately showpiece in the garden. While I fully enjoy this site, my heart is even more attracted to another aspect related to its three distinct phases: a bloom period in early summer, a time where the plant dies off, and then a rejuvenated bloom period in the autumn. Can you see the comparison? Jesus lived, he died, and he overcame death in wonderful resurrection. The delphinium is a wonderful representation of resurrection.

A Love Gift from God

Sometimes as tall as five feet or even taller, the upright delphinium is majestic in the garden. With two distinct bloom periods, the first lasts nearly two months in early summer where a strong wind can prematurely knock the giant flowers over. If the wind does not catch them, the center leader of the flower dies first and is soon followed by the secondary branches.

In mid-summer, the stalks that carried the full and gorgeous blooms have completely died off. With the plant appearing dead or nearly dead, a second set of leaves begins to develop at the base so that by late summer, the next round of blossoms may have as much or even more beauty as the first. These second blossoms may last an additional two months and are often the last flowers to die off as a result of a heavy freeze.

The analogy between the three phases of the delphinium and of Christ is perhaps easily understood. The life, death, and then resurrection of Jesus has been the central message of many, many sermons. The focus of these messages may be the miracle of his resurrection, sometimes it is a look at the suffering that he endured for our sake, and most frequently it is an encouragement for people to accept Christ as their Savior.

It seems appropriate that in this book on love that we remember that Christ died because of love:

> *But God is so rich in mercy, and he loved us so much, that even though we were dead because of our sins, he gave us life when he raised Christ from the dead. (It is only by God's grace that you have been saved!) ... God saved you by his grace when you believed. And you can't take credit for this; it is a gift from God* (Ephesians 2:4,5,8).

The suffering that Christ endured, his death, and then the miracle of his resurrection was a love gift! We didn't ask for it because we had not even been born – it was a gift that preceded us by many, many years.

Why this particular love gift from God? He wanted to be re-united with us. For years the Lord had been separated from us because of the foolishness of Adam and Eve. This gift is the *"incredible wealth of his grace and kindness toward us ... [for we] ... are united with Christ Jesus"* (Ephesians 2:7). This separation ended when we said "YES!" to the Lord.

The delphinium is therefore not just a showy plant that serves as a reminder of the life, death, and then resurrection of Jesus – it is also a reminder of this tremendous love gift that he offers to us so we can be bound together with him.

A Garden of Love

Flax and Soapwort

My heart melted when I first saw the harmoniously pleasing flax and soapwart together at a garden store. Unfortunately, the delicacy of these colors is hard to capture in a photograph. With these two plants, I felt at such peace as the soft pink soapwort was combined with the true blue flax. It brought to my mind the harmony with one another that is God's plan for each of us: *"Live in harmony with each other"* (Romans 12:16).

Harmony

In a band or orchestra, when all of the instruments play in the same harmonic sequences, a soothing effect is achieved that is pleasing to the ear and is greater than the individual instruments could present. The great meals that are prepared by the finest restaurants are the combination of tastes, flavors, and delicacies that well exceed the individual piece of meat, vegetable, fruit, or pasta. The gentle breeze that comes off a lake on a summer evening is refreshingly cool as it passes over our warmer bodies. Harmony is how various disparate objects are put together in a synergistic manner to create an aesthetically pleasing sense or aroma with an increased effect.

The pink soapwort has masses of delicate blossoms that are low to the ground with one-half inch flowers. The beautiful blue flax, being somewhat taller, complements the soapwort in height, form, and color – the delicate pink and soft blue blossoms, both of roughly the same size, present a satisfying and enjoyable effect for the viewer.

Lack of harmony is contrary to God's will. How often have we heard the degradation of one faith, denomination or theology over another? Though some are more vocal than others, we can hear it from Catholics, Protestants, Baptists, Pentecostals, Episcopalians, Seventh Day Adventists, Presbyterians, and many more. Each has their flavor or twist on Christianity, each presenting their view or understanding based on the revelation that they have received and the tradition of their forefathers. Each can turn to the Bible to support their faith arguments.

Harmony recognizes that we don't know it all. Harmony allows for grace because our understanding may be imperfect. Harmony understands that the theology that we have today is more refined than it was yesterday. Harmony allows for each person to continue to develop and receive a new revelation from God. Harmony hopes for everyone to refine their spiritual maturity, removing what is wrong, and developing what is right.

> *For the Kingdom of God is … living a life of goodness and peace and joy in the Holy Spirit. If you serve Christ with this attitude, you will please God, and others will approve of you, too. So then, let us aim for harmony in the church and try to build each other up* (Romans 14:17-19).

In this translation, the words *"in the church"* were added by the Bible translators in an attempt to help us understand that these words were addressed to the body of Christ as individuals and congregations alike. That is, harmony between all believers.

If we are to truly love one another, Jesus wants to replace our arrogance and prideful thinking with compassion, understanding, and grace. If we suspect that a person has the wrong theology, we can certainly pray that the Lord will open the spiritual eyes of the person that has the wrong thinking, whether it is ourselves or the other person. Love hopes for the revelation of everyone to a fuller understanding of the Kingdom of God. That is harmony.

The flax and the soapwort are just one example of flower combinations that seem to work very well together, and there are many, some even better that these two. The hope is for harmonious oneness in Christ, for the Kingdom of God is at hand.

A Garden of Love

Forget-Me-Not

I selected the forget-me-not for the garden because it speaks to me about loving relationships. These simple light-blue petals paint the mid-spring garden, each with five miniature brush strokes clustered around a center. In the forget-me-not, I see elegance and intimacy wrapped together in love – here it expresses our intimate relationship with Jesus.

Deep and Intimate Love

The forget-me-not is one of the few perennials in northern climates that have true light-blue flowers with complimentary light green leaves. Standing only as tall as one's ankles with tiny flowers that are as delicate as fine lace, it somehow brings thoughts of a properly set table with exquisite tea, chocolate-raspberry truffles for two, and pleasing conversations. On that table are delicately decorated china plates, white linen napkins and a silver candlestick that emits enough light so that the intimacy of the moment may be enjoyed. Oh how great is our Lord!

The delicate forget-me-not radiates a certain happiness and contentment – "Please stay here just a little longer, I so appreciate our time together." It seems to say with all sincerity, "Can you tell me about … ", and so the conversation goes on for a while longer.

Intimacy may be one of the hardest concepts to describe, possibly because it is so profound. Intimate conversations can ensue, yet no audible sounds would necessarily be spoken. In it are the heartaches, the joys, the successes and failures of our children, our hopes, trials, pains, and yes of course our love.

Intimacy may be with a spouse, a parent, some other relative, or a best friend. The most intimate of relationships is intended to be with our Lord. Even the disciples that spent so much time with Jesus did not want him to die because they feared that their relationship would be lost. How truly fortunate, how truly blessed, we are that he went away for only a very short while.

Jesus said,

> *"Don't let your hearts be troubled. Trust in God, and trust also in me"*
> (John 14:1).

Later in the same chapter, Jesus explained how that depth of intimacy was possible.

> *"When I am raised to life again, you will know that I am in my Father, and you are in me, and I am in you … And because they love me, my Father will love them"* (John 14:20,21).

The intimacy with Christ, that very close and personal relationship with the only Son of the Father, is made possible because we truly and deeply love the Lord, allowing Christ to be in us and ourselves in Christ.

The scientist says "How is this possible?" while those that have significantly progressed in their faith have understood and experienced this, not on a physical level, but spiritually. Our Lord listens to us and he speaks to us, knowing fully the depths of our situations, because *"Nothing can ever separate us from God's love"* (Romans 8:38).

In this sense, the dainty forget-me-not is suggestive of the deeply profound love that is found by taking the time, allowing ourselves to relax, yield, and become supple – that we can profoundly receive this intimacy with our loving Lord, Jesus Christ, who so thoroughly wants every part of us.

Gaura

Each year I purchase at least one perennial that I am not familiar with – the gaura is one such example, and what a find! While I marvel at these pink and white flowers for their long-lasting delicacy, I am deeply inspired by their movement on a still day. Even on seemingly windless days, the flower heads gently sway back and forth, moved by a breeze that cannot be seen or felt, as a reminder of the Holy Spirit's presence.

The Holy Spirit Helps Us Love

Plant lovers have joyfully admired the long-lasting and delicate gaura flowers, noting their ability to "dance in the breeze." On windless days, even on the stillest of days, the tall wand-like flowers are gently moved from side to side by some invisible power, one that cannot be seen or felt. Try as we might to identify that force, whether it is the breath of wind or the heat from the sun's rays that we don't recognize, we can only marvel at this incredible mystery.

When the breeze is more distinct, the long stemmed airy flowers appear like little pink or white butterflies that are attempting to be free from their tether. The slender two or three foot stems give it the "wand flower" name, yet each stem is strong enough to carry the weight of its flower while bending with each puff of wind. Although the gaura completely dies back in the winter, new green or purple growth in the spring produces the first blossoms by early summer – they continue their profuse and ethereal effect through the last color of the fall.

The gaura seems to understand that even on the hottest, driest, and stillest of days, the gentle wind is present. On those days where we walk into the garden, spent from the challenges, chaos, and difficulties of our worlds, we can walk to the gaura to see it moving, oh so lovingly and peacefully, in the wind.

The gaura knows the wind, but it also seems to know the spirit. In the Scriptures, the same Hebrew word is used for wind and spirit. For example, this word *ruwach* was used in the liberating story of the exodus from Egypt. The Lord brought an east wind so that the waters of the sea were divided:

> *Then Moses raised his hand over the sea, and the* Lord *opened up a path through the water with a strong east wind* **[ruwach]**. *The wind blew all that night, turning the seabed into dry land* (Exodus 14:21).

This word *ruwach* is also translated as spirit in other Old Testament locations:

> *Joshua son of Nun was full of the spirit* **[ruwach]** *of wisdom* (Deuteronomy 34:9).

As the Israelites reached the sea during the Exodus, it could have been translated "*and the* Lord *caused the sea to open by a strong spirit from the east all that night and made the sea dry and divided the waters*" (author's translation).

Therefore, as the gaura flowers dance in the wind, they can remind us of the presence of the Holy Spirit. The wind and the spirit were much more closely interchangeable in Old Testament times than they are today.

What does this have to do with love? Consider this verse regarding one of the roles of the Holy Spirit:

> *We know how dearly God loves us, because he has given us the Holy Spirit to fill our hearts with his love* (Romans 5:5).

One purpose of the Holy Spirit is to help us to be effective in demonstrating his love.

The gaura knows the wind is there, reminding us that the wind is still present. But even more, they remind us and help restore us to a place where we can more effectively love through the filling grace of the Holy Spirit.

Grape Hyacinth

The grape hyacinth, with its white, cobalt blue, and violet colors, somehow reminds me of little Smurfs. Do you remember the *Smurfs*, a children's cartoon from two decades ago? Some people see the miniature clusters as beads or grapes – I see obedient little Smurfs. I remember how the Smurfs showed love for each other, but mostly I remember their obedience.

Obedience to Christ

In the spring, the grape hyacinths are among the various bulbs that come joyously popping forth out of the ground. They bloom at approximately the same time as the bright yellow daffodils yet they are not nearly as tall. After a long winter, both plants suggest a new beginning as they are raised to a new life.

Unlike the fragrant and more popular hyacinth which is not related, the grape hyacinth has many tiny round white, blue and purple balls that are tightly organized around a central stem. Each ball is a blossom in itself, each having a balloon-like or grape-like appearance. When planted in mass, which is the recommended procedure, they appear as little blue Smurfs that are obediently following their teacher on a field trip.

Just as the Smurfs were obedient little creatures, so too are Christians explicitly instructed to be obedient:

> *"If you love me, obey my commandments"* (John 14:15).

Remembering that the first commandment is to love the Lord your God, this verse is calling for obedience as a necessary condition. If your husband (that is Christ) asks you for something, do it out of love – here, the emphasis is on what Jesus has commanded. Jesus continued this thought after a few verses:

> *"Those who accept my commandments and obey them are the ones who love me. And because they love me, my Father will love them. And I will love them and reveal myself to each of them"* (John 14:21).

Jesus continued:

> *"All who love me will do what I say.* My Father will love them, and we will come and make our home with each of them. Anyone who doesn't love me will not obey me" (John 14:23,24).

In 1 John, further clarification is provided:

> If someone claims, "I know God," but doesn't obey God's commandments, that person is a liar and is not living in the truth. But those who obey God's word truly show how completely they love him (1 John 2:4,5).

Here is the point. When we love one another, we are to show acts of kindness, compassion, forgiveness, mercy, humility, and so on. WHEN WE LOVE THE LORD, WE INTENTIONALLY OBEY. Love expects obedience – when that happens, these verses promise a deep and profound response of love for God.

Help us Lord to be obedient to you, and help us see in ourselves those areas where we are blind to our own disobedience. Lord, we want the fullness of your love – help us to dwell in that love and to remain in that love. Thank you, dear Lord Jesus. Amen.

A Garden of Love

Honeysuckle Vine

Outstanding! I am so captivated by this most intricate and lovely vine. Do you see the little two-inch long pink trumpets? I can imagine hearing them boldly declare their warmest greeting, "Enter, for the Lord is in this place, offering peace to you!" As Paul wrote many times in his epistles, *"May God our Father and the Lord Jesus Christ give you grace and peace"* (Ephesians 1:2).

Peace

One of the loveliest of the newer plants to be introduced in many years is the ornate trumpet honeysuckle vine, hybridized with other twining honeysuckles to create a flower of immense beauty. Elongated tubes of either rosy-pink or pastel-orange are offset with a soft cream colored throat, more intricate than any glass blower could prepare. The stamens and pistil protrudes in an extended form from the trumpet-shaped throat in hopes of luring a passing insect as an open invitation for pollination. The many trumpets seem to be calling out to both the insect and the garden visitor, "Come and enter in, welcome to a special place, a place of new beginnings, a place of satisfaction and peace."

All of the varieties of honeysuckle vines grow tall, often up to twenty or twenty-five feet, as they search for full sun on a strong supporting structure. Some vines are more fragrant than others – the European honeysuckle is considered the sweetest. The hummingbirds with their long needle-like beak seem to particularly enjoy the nectar from all the twining honeysuckles vines, darting from flower to flower, from cluster to cluster.

If the honeysuckle vine is positioned at the entrance to the garden, the trumpet-shaped flowers seem to herald the visitor, "You are about to enter a most special place." In some ways this is reminiscent of the armies of angels at the birth of Jesus, *"praising God and saying, 'Glory to God in the highest heaven, and peace on earth to those with whom God is pleased'"* (Luke 2:13,14). The peace and presence of our Lord is in the garden.

Jesus came to earth to give a gift of peace, and his expectation was and is that the gift would be used. *"I am leaving you with a gift – peace of mind and heart. And the peace I give is a gift the world cannot give. So don't be troubled or afraid"* (John 14:27). Then, only a few days later, that gift was received.

> *'Peace be with you,' he said. As he spoke, he showed them the wounds in his hands and his side. They were filled with joy when they saw the Lord! Again he said, 'Peace be with you. As the Father has sent me, so I am sending you.' Then he breathed on them and said, 'Receive the Holy Spirit'* (John 20:19-22).

These verses indicate that the gift of the Holy Spirit is a gift of peace. Many times the Scriptures associate the Holy Spirit with power – the power of supernatural healing, for example. Here, however, the peace that the Holy Spirit brings is peace of mind and heart in oneness with God – this deep fellowship is one that is immersed in love.

> *Be joyful. Grow to maturity. Encourage each other. Live in harmony and peace. Then the God of love and peace will be with you* (2 Corinthians 13:11).

Hyssop

I thoroughly enjoy showing visitors to the garden the anise hyssop, pointing out its Scriptural significance. These profuse flowers, reminiscent of the Biblical hyssop plant, help us visualize the final moments of Christ's suffering. Each plant has an abundance of bluish-purple flowers, like many paintbrushes.

Love in Action

The anise hyssop develops its first set of leaves in the early springtime, having the pleasing and nostalgic aroma of licorice that might have been stored in grandma's candy jar. By the time mid-summer arrives, honey bees are attracted to the same aroma on the profuse lavender-blue flower heads that extend like many paintbrushes ready to be dipped. Slowly the flowers change to blue-gray so that eventually by winter, a strong and hardened plant remains as a reminder of its previous glory.

Botanists have struggled with identifying the specific hyssop plant that is mentioned in the Bible. The most popular suggestion is a white-flowered bush that grows abundantly in dry, rocky locations. The anise hyssop, with its spires of bluish-purple flowers, is in the same mint family as that white-flowered hyssop bush, but is a distant cousin.

In the moments before the death of Christ, the hyssop carried the wine vinegar to his lips (John 19:28-30). Jesus had stated he was thirsty, so a sponge, full of bitter wine vinegar, was placed on the hyssop and then presented to Jesus.

> *A jar of sour wine was sitting there, so they soaked a sponge in it, put it on a hyssop branch, and held it up to his lips. When Jesus had tasted it, he said, "It is finished!" Then he bowed his head and released his spirit* (John 19:29,30).

When the old sour wine was put to Jesus' lips, it failed to satisfy him and he rejected it stating *"It is finished!"* He had provided new wine at Cana in the hope that some would trust and believe in him (John 2:1-12), but these men mockingly offered sour old wine (Luke 23:36). Disappointed, Jesus knew his time on earth was finished and he released his spirit.

Contrast this story with the familiar story of the Good Samaritan. Jesus had asked a religious expert how he reads the Law, to which he replied *"'You must love the LORD your God with all your heart, all your soul, all your strength, and all your mind.' And, 'Love your neighbor as yourself'"* (Luke 10:27). Jesus then told the parable of the Samaritan that had compassion for an injured and beaten man. Here, the Samaritan extended himself by soothing the man's wounds, taking him to a better place, and then, assured he would be taken care of, continued on his way.

Mercy is offering our best to those who need it. The Samaritan showed great amounts of mercy to the injured man: he soothed, transported, and provided for him. Later in the Book of Luke, Jesus said,

> *"Blessed are all who hear the word of God and put it into practice"*
> (Luke 11:28).

Mercy is love in action. The hyssop was misused by the soldiers by extending an inferior wine to Jesus, but the good Samaritan put his love into practice. May we each extend our best to others in mercy and love.

Iris

I am deeply touched by the grace shown in the spectacular Siberian iris, like an intricate and elegant bouquet. The blossoms normally have three types of petals: falls that point downwards, stylearms that are immediately above the falls, and standards that point up. Each blossom seems to say what Jesus said to Paul,

"My grace is all you need" (2 Corinthians 12:9).

Grace

Hurriedly we have passed by a place – time after time, the beauty of the moment has completely escaped us – until one day, a fragrance rises or the sun radiates or the dew sparkles or the bird sings. Suddenly we stop, "How did I miss that?" we ask, but we know that the surprise encounter is intended to slow us down, to catch something that has been appointed for that moment. Can we afford the time? God has set us aside to capture another essence of himself – we know that the Lord is doing something unique, for it is time once again to catch a glimpse of his grace.

The surprise of the Siberian iris can be one such encounter – strolling through the late spring garden can reveal an exhilarating look at how the Lord weaves simple plant matter into a most delicate and ornate creation. Three-inch bright flowers, purple, blue, pink, occasionally white or yellow, suddenly appear before us and our breath is taken away. Lord, you are so very good! Your grace is all we need.

In early spring, clusters of simple yet elongated grass-like leaves begin reaching for the sky, taking two months before they open. The leaves would never let us suspect the intricacy of these open-faced flowers with nine petals: three lower downward facing petals called "falls" because they fall or bend towards the ground, three "stylearms" that shield the base of the "falls", and three upper arching petals known as "standards." The falls, stylearms, and standards may be of one color or they may be in breathtaking contrast – either way, their elegance represents how well grace, when offered, can be received.

The grace that is suggested by the iris may be attributed to a balance between the falls, stylearms, and the standards. Grace infers falling or bending downward because, based on past performance, the subsequent action may not be merited. The stylearms cover the past performance with abundant forgiveness. The standards suggest an expression of hope as they look up at what should be and hopefully will come. In this sense, grace might be thought of as an interesting balance between humility, forgiveness, and hope: humbling ourselves despite failures of the past (the falls), forgiving the past (the stylearms), and passionately hoping for something better (the standards).

Grace is favor, ignoring who the person is or what they have done. That favor is humbly offered, putting aside those things that may have happened. The favor is presented with hope but not with an expectation – there may never be a positive response and that is perfectly ok. Grace recognizes that the kindness which is offered may not be deserved, but it is extended anyway. Grace is extended as a blessing.

While it is recognized that God has granted grace to born-again Christians, the sense here is that grace is for us to offer in the same way to others. Forgiveness is that portion of grace that ignores the past, putting it behind us. Kindness is that portion of grace that propels us forward in hope.
Note how Peter's words compel us to increased grace:

> *May God give you more and more grace and peace as you grow in your knowledge of God and Jesus our Lord* (2 Peter 1:2).

The result is God-given grace, extended in humility, forgiveness, and kindness to those that may or may not deserve it. As the iris suggests, may God give us increased grace and peace – may we know God and Jesus more and more intimately.

A Garden of Love

Jacob's Ladder

I am grateful and humbled by the opportunity to develop this garden, putting together design concepts as an expression of my personal vision of peace, serenity, and the presence of our Lord. My choice to keep yellow colors out of the garden during the summer and fall months, for example, is controversial, yet is consistent with how I view the softness of God's love. It is my hope and desire that people are touched in this garden, feeling the love of God's presence. The Jacob's ladder is one such landscaping design piece.

Controlled by the Holy Spirit

The most popular landscaped gardens are those that seem to flow well together, mixing patterns, repeating patterns, applying the unexpected, and adding areas of intimacy. When developing a new flower bed or garden area, landscapers recommend developing a vision of the setting including an anticipation of where the largest plant or plants will appear. If people are to view the planting area from all directions, the largest plant should be placed somewhere near the center of the flower bed. When the bed is to back up to a fence or a building, the largest plants should be placed behind all other plants so that each can be properly viewed. In this way, the design builds towards a point starting with the smallest along the border, then taller plants, and then finally the tallest – at least three levels of height seem to give the bed an aesthetically pleasing distinction to the viewing eye.

One exception to this design approach uses an effect called a "scrim" which allows a taller plant to be placed in the front of the flower border. In the theater, a scrim is a thin cotton-like curtain that is placed near the front of the stage – by adjusting the stage lighting, those objects behind the scrim can either be hidden or revealed. In landscaping, by placing a light and airy plant along the border, people can enjoy the border plant and also see beyond the scrim and into the flower bed, even if plants behind it are shorter.

The Jacob's ladder, decorated in elegant purplish blue plumes, is one such airy plant that can be positioned as a scrim with shorter plants behind. By carefully controlling the number of plants so that the effect is not too thick, the complementary colors and textures that are behind may be pleasantly enjoyed while looking through the screen.

As with the scrim on the border, too many plants may represent inward focused individuals who want attention focused on themselves or their selfish needs – this is the sinful nature. Properly spaced plants, on the other hand, represent how our Christian minds should be controlled by the Holy Spirit. The question is, do we focus on ourselves and what we want, or do we see others and their needs as we are led by God's Spirit?

The issue boils down to which spiritual force will control our minds.

> *Letting your sinful nature control your mind leads to death. But letting the Spirit control your mind leads to life and peace. For the sinful nature is always hostile to God. It never did obey God's laws, and it never will. That's why those who are still under the control of their sinful nature can never please God* (Romans 8:6-8).

One of the purposes of the Holy Spirit is to help control our minds. If we are born-again Christians, we have the Holy Spirit within us to help us control what we are not able to control on our own. Yet we have to yield to that Spirit.

> *Don't use your freedom to satisfy your sinful nature. Instead, use your freedom to serve one another in love ... So I say, let the Holy Spirit guide your lives. Then you won't be doing what your sinful nature craves* (Galatians 5:13,16).

The thin scrim-like veil of the Jacob's ladder should help remind us and empower us to be victorious over our sinful, selfish nature, allowing the Holy Spirit to control our minds and guide our lives in love for one another.

A Garden of Love

Lamb's Ear

Soft as a satin blouse, the skin of a newborn baby, a cotton ball, a child's stuffed bunny rabbit, a velvet jacket, or a peachskin dress – such is the gentleness of the lamb's ear. Our Christ has that same gentleness and even more – Scriptures call us to demonstrate our love and gentleness in the same way.

Gentleness

The ambiance of a garden is not dependent on just one lovely flower, flowing conifer, or curvaceous walkway, but rather on the total effect that the collection suggests. The delphinium can add its elegant stateliness; the Siberian iris its soft grace; the columbine its friendly kindness; and the rose its peaceful splendor. The textures of each soothing, simple, polite, joyous, or gregarious variety help develop the overall aura as do the changing color themes be they bright yellows, deep purples, hot pinks, intense reds, gentle whites, or soft blues. The whole is far greater than the individual parts.

The lamb's ear has exceptionally soft leaves, silvery-gray patches of thick velvet that cover one another with a soothing and restful effect. In the late spring, flower stalks with pink subtle buds reach above the leaves in a simplistic form. The plants are surprisingly aggressive as they take up more territory, which may seem inconsistent when compared to their otherwise gentle character. Or is it that they are attempting to spread their gentleness?

Just as the astilbe suggests the humility and gentleness of Christ, so the lamb's ear can suggest the same should be true for us. Paul wrote to the Ephesians:

> *Always be humble and gentle. Be patient with each other, making allowance for each other's faults because of your love. Make every effort to keep yourselves united in the Spirit, binding yourselves together with peace* (Ephesians 4:2,3).

Gentleness, when combined with other attributes such as patience, kindness, goodness, faithfulness, self-control, tenderness, and compassion, helps build the ambiance of love.

Elsie knew that her time on earth was near an end – she had congestive heart failure and her kidneys were shutting down as she lay in her hospital bed with her husband George at her side. At 92 years old, she still had the same sweetness that George remembered when they were first married seventy-one years earlier. Elsie began the conversation, "George, do you remember all those adorable stuffed lambs that I sewed and then gave to the orphanages?"

Of course George remembered – how could he forget? Elsie frequently went to an upstairs bedroom that was converted to a sewing room, bringing out the white lambskin-looking plush fabric along with black plush for the nose, ears, and eyes. She first started using cotton balls for the stuffing, but in later years she switched to polyfil because it was nearly as soft and was non-allergenic. The lambs were so huggable, so cuddly, so lovable.

Elsie continued, "George, years ago I made a special one for you, bigger than all the others, and I have saved it so I could give it to you now." He wondered what this was all about but did not say a word because he had mellowed significantly. Her weak voice strained, "Did you ever wonder why I sewed so many lambs?" He nodded; she handed him a large plastic bag. "Just after we were married, my grandmother told me the secret of a happy marriage was to never argue. She taught me to keep quiet in my anger, and to make those adorable little lambs instead. One particular day was very difficult for me, so I prayed to God that he would make you into that soft lamb. Today, George, I can see that you have become what I prayed for. Please accept this gift of my love for you."

> *Pursue righteousness and a godly life, along with faith, love, perseverance, and gentleness* (1 Timothy 6:11).

A Garden of Love

Lavender

Can you recall the lush fragrance of lavender? These sprays of purple and blue lavender reach out, greeting us with a fragrance that is both romantic and peaceful. Our senses are filled by this refreshing aroma as we breathe deeply their fresh scent, similar to the pleasing aroma of Christ's love.

A Pleasing Fragrance

Richly fragrant leaves and flowers delight the garden path – heavenly aromas that saturate our senses with a sweet smell that has been enjoyed for many, many years. Gently rub one of the gray-green leaves, breathing in the unforgettably pleasant scent. Even the scent of lavender seems soft, pleasing, and delicate – an aroma that satisfies and lingers, until we say "More, please?"

English lavender is a shorter plant with blue or deep violet flowers, French lavender is a larger plant with purple flowers and is sometimes called 'sweet lavender', and hybrid lavenders, such as that shown on the opposite page, are appropriate for cooler regions. Lavenders require a well-drained location such as a slope where water will run off during the winter; all of the lavender varieties are very fragrant.

Some roses are very pleasantly scented, as are Russian sage, hyacinth, lily-of-the valley, phlox, and many other flowers. Trees and shrubs can be equally fragrant – lilac, cedar, fragrant viburnum, spruce, hemlock, and many others. Certainly the herbs, such as rosemary, basil, thyme, and sage, are well known for their culinary flavoring and sweet odors. Each scent, fragrance, and flavoring is a unique way of expressing the individual plant.

In some respects, how we express our love can be compared to fragrances – some with more delicacy, some with greater sweetness, and some being more robust. To those people that need Christ as their Savior, they interact with us and observe our fragrance. Jesus said,

> *"Your love for one another will prove to the world that you are my disciples"*
> (John 13:35).

As one Christian writer put it, "You may be the closest that many people get to a church." Our fragrance emits, our light shines, our love gives, our touch reveals.

The way we present ourselves to those we work with, we shop with, we live with, we pray with, we see at the movies or restaurants or church – that is a representation of our fragrant love of our Lord. As Paul wrote to the Corinthians,

> *He* [God] *uses us to spread the knowledge of Christ everywhere, like a sweet perfume. Our lives are a Christ-like fragrance rising up to God. But this fragrance is perceived differently by those who are being saved and by those who are perishing. To those who are perishing, we are a dreadful smell of death and doom. But to those who are being saved, we are a life-giving perfume* (2 Corinthians 2:14-16).

Oh the fragrant lavender – every whiff, every breath, every molecule of loving essence, enjoying and allowing it to permeate our souls. Our love is to be that essence; our lives being that Christ-like fragrance that rises up to God.

A Garden of Love

Lily

Jesus said "And why worry about your clothing? Look at the lilies of the field and how they grow" *(Matthew 6:28).*

Trust the Lord

Resurrection Sunday is traditionally the day of the loveliest of women's outfits – floral pastels, sunshine yellows, passionate purples, and serene blues, each with ruffled, embroidered, sequined, beaded, or pearled accents. One by one, they walk into the church's sanctuary only to be taken back by the surprising beauty of the ultra-white Easter lily, *Lilium longiflorum*. Just as Jesus' resurrection stunned those who knew of his crucifixion, so the Easter lily greets the congregation with its sudden appearance. A few days earlier, people were talking of his suffering and ultimately his death; now, the song is *"He's Alive"* – these funnel-shaped pure white lilies symbolize his new life.

A considerable amount of controversy surrounds what is the *"lilies of the field"* from Matthew 6:28 and Luke 12:27. Some suggest that the Madonna lily, *Lilium candidum*, is that plant and then use the Easter lily, shown on the opposite page, due to its striking similarity; many Biblical plant scholars rather suspect that the *"lilies of the field"* refers to a red-flowered anemone that appears far more frequently throughout Israel. Either way, the lilies and the anemones are bulbous plants, and that is the important consideration regarding the teaching on *"lilies of the field"*:

> *"Look at the lilies and how they grow. They don't work or make their clothing, yet Solomon in all his glory was not dressed as beautifully as they are. And if God cares so wonderfully for flowers that are here today and thrown into the fire tomorrow, he will certainly care for you. Why do you have so little faith?"* (Luke 12:27,28).

The challenge that Jesus was suggesting is "Look again at how the lilies grow."

Lilies, anemones, tulips, and cyclamen each have bulbs or tubers that are built into their root structure that provide a reserve supply of nutrients during drought periods. In a land where a drought can last for multiple years, the ability for a tuberous or bulbous plant to survive in Israel during their difficult times was critical. Therefore, the tubers are not seen by the naked eye yet they provide for the survival of the plant.

The tubers also helped when the plant was *"thrown into the fire."* The practice in many nations is to build a fire after the harvest is completed, fully consuming the excess plant material in preparation for the next season's planting. Any lilies that were growing above the surface were burned, but to their surprise, new lily plants sprouted quickly because the tubers, located several inches below the ground surface, were deep enough to ensure that the heat of the fire would not harm them.

As Jesus taught this lesson, the drought and fire appear as symbolic representations of trials that people go through:

> *These trials will show that your faith is genuine. It is being tested as fire tests and purifies gold – though your faith is far more precious than mere gold. … You love him even though you have never seen him. Though you do not see him now, you trust him; and you rejoice with a glorious, inexpressible joy. The reward for trusting him will be the salvation of your souls* (1 Peter 1:7,8).

The lesson of the lilies is this – if God so wonderfully provides tubers to lilies and such plants, won't he do even more for us? Trust and love the Lord because he is gushing and overflowing with love for us – that is the lesson of the lilies.

A Garden of Love

Marsh Marigold

I so very much appreciate the help that volunteers have given in developing and maintaining this garden. One volunteer was a young man named Lukas from Germany that helped for nearly four months. Faithfully for many days, Lukas cleared a large area near the stream bed, planting it with ferns and marsh marigolds. The result was breath-taking as the marsh marigolds filled the stream banks with their intense yellow flowers. I am so thankful for this faithful working companion.

Faith

Suddenly for two weeks in the spring, the wetlands become like a field of sparkling gold as the marsh marigolds display their sunny yellow blooms. The marsh marigold is a naturally-found perennial flower that grows abundantly in the muck of swampy areas and along stream beds in cooler zones of northeastern United States. Once they are done flowering, they grow inconspicuously in their natural habitat for the balance of the growing season. While this yellow-flowered beauty shares the same name as the annual marigold, the two plants are not related.

Plants that grow along stream beds and other very wet locations have very different root requirements than those of the perennial garden. The leaves begin sprouting as the water becomes warmer in very early spring. After two weeks of flowering, the warming spring and then the summer heat can cause the roots to dry out as the heart-shaped leaves become almost insignificant. Once the moisture returns in the fall, the roots can spend five months completely submerged underwater. To the marsh marigold, faith is the ability to live through an extended dormant period, waiting for its short green cycle.

About faith, the Scriptures state that *"Faith is the confidence that what we hope for will actually happen; it gives us assurance about things we cannot see"* (Hebrews 11:1). The marsh marigold seems to understand that as the frigid waters of winter become slightly warmer, the long wait is finally coming to an end.

Regarding love and faith, the Scriptures also state *"God showed his great love for us by sending Christ to die for us while we were still sinners"* (Romans 5:8). God did it because he is head-over-heals in love with us, no matter who we are or what we have done. He is so in love that he wants to actually dwell within us. To do so, however, God has some housekeeping to attend to and that process begins with faith: *"People are made right with God when they believe that Jesus sacrificed his life, shedding his blood"* (Romans 3:25).

Faith then says it is willing to give up control of those things that are abhorrent to God, turning over control to the Holy Spirit. *"You are controlled by the Spirit if you have the Spirit of God living in you"* (Romans 8:9). Faith gives assurance about things we cannot see.

To the greatly forgiven woman that poured expensive perfume on Jesus, he said, *"She has shown me much love"* (Luke 7:47). Her exceptional faith motivated this extraordinary act of love. The marsh marigold gives the example of exceptional faith by living in dormancy for an extended period, only to bloom for just two weeks. Paul, in his letter to the Galatians, wrote, *"What is important is faith expressing itself in love"* (Galatians 5:6).

Phlox

One evening at dusk while the phlox were in full bloom, I stood for a long time meditating about this flower. It was late and I could only make out shadows, but some flying insect or moth appeared to be drinking from the very, very fragrant phlox flowers. In and out it darted, yet I could not make out what it was. Then there were several, each doing the same. Finally I saw their long beak and I knew instantly – baby hummingbirds. Encouraged by this, I excitedly called home to tell my wife.

Encouragement

Sometimes an encouraging word is all we need so that we will continue pressing on – the garden phlox seems to grab our attention, enthusiastically suggesting, "I have confidence in you." The warmth, the friendliness, and the fullness all appear to repeat the same thing, "You are God's chosen – he chose you!" Out of the awesome display of color and the fullness of growth, the words seem to come forth, "You may condemn yourself, but I see your goodness and your worth."

With masses of small, star-shaped, colorful flowers blanketing the plants, the garden phlox are a sight to behold. Each year, the number of perennial phlox increases with new and more intriguing varieties: subtle pink, patient purple, encouraging red, pure white, rich violet, and even pale gray. With such a plethora of color and fullness, the richness can be joyfully exclamatory, pleasingly satisfying, or peacefully relaxing.

This easy-to-grow perennial seems bound and determined to produce and then produce again. Each plant, with its many flower stalks, may be cut back when they are short in the spring for more branching and heavier flowering. Cut them back again after they have blossomed for even more color. Some years, phlox have been known to bloom from mid-June through September or October.

The many flower stalks of each plant and the long season of blossoms illustrate how repetition is essential to be an effective encourager. When massed together, these full blooming flowers boldly repeat their heartening message. The author of Hebrews wrote,

> *Let us think of ways to motivate one another to acts of love and good works* (Hebrews 10:24).

The encourager understands that God purposely moves him or her on in their walk as lovers of the Lord and one another. Our Lord does not want carnality, he wants vigor and life – he does not want defeat, he wants victory. The encourager understands God's goal as well as the importance of communicating that goal.

The encourager also knows the importance of boldly pursuing the presence of God. Hebrews states,

> *And since we have a great High Priest who rules over God's house, let us go right into the presence of God with sincere hearts fully trusting him. For our guilty consciences have been sprinkled with Christ's blood to make us clean* (Hebrews 10:21,22).

Guilt and self-condemnation are tools that the enemy uses to keep us from our Lord, the central location of love. The encourager understands that feelings of self-worthlessness result in distancing ourselves from God, while also recognizing that the one who fully and sincerely trusts will achieve close proximity to the Lord. The encourager repeats and then repeats again so that trust builds upon trust and love builds upon love.

The phlox also shows us the risk that is at hand, for the encourager realizes that some will turn away from God's love, oftentimes through discouragement:

> *But we are not like those who turn away from God to their own destruction. We are the faithful ones, whose souls will be saved* (Hebrews 10:39).

A Garden of Love

Primrose

My friend Lukas took this photo of the primrose. He enjoyed how it is simple and unassuming with a modest and lowly yet cheery presentation. Throughout the Scriptures, there are many stories and directives that call for us to give up our pride and to take on a spirit of humility. Lukas continually showed his gentle and humble spirit.

Humility

In a non-assuming and unpretentious manner, the primroses are the first flowers to appear in the frigid garden in the spring. Timidly, hints of purple, yellow, white, pink, orange, or vermilion peak their heads above the ground while scattered layers of snow still linger between the flowers. Seemingly these short, modestly appointed flowers ask "If it pleases you, Mr. Spring, I would like your permission to start displaying my colors."

While roses and primroses share their similarity of name, they are not at all related. The roses ornately appear above woody, thorn-filled branches while the simple primrose develops with short, supple stems. Some rose varieties are only one foot tall but most are considerably taller, possibly even ten or twelve feet. The primroses appear content with being only three or four inches high.

The downfall of many people in the Bible can be attributed to a lack of humility. Hezekiah showed off the wealth in the temple to the Babylonians which ultimately contributed to the downfall of Judah. Ananias and Sapphira could have avoided their problems by humbly admitting their actions. The devil, when tempting Eve, appealed to her pride. Prior to his conversion, even Paul referred to himself as a very arrogant man.

There are many verses that instruct us to be humble – here are two:

> *As the Scriptures say, 'God opposes the proud but favors the humble.' So humble yourselves before God* (James 4:6,7).

And:

> *While knowledge makes us feel important, it is love that strengthens the church. Anyone who claims to know all the answers doesn't really know very much. But the person who loves God is the one whom God recognizes* (1 Corinthians 8:1-3).

Humility is having an unassuming position and a lack of aggressiveness, boastfulness and self-righteousness; humility is modesty, lacking pride or arrogance; humility allows others to do the exalting.

The primrose, though rich in bright colors, has that simple, unassuming stature.

A Garden of Love

Rose

Oh the exquisite rose! I take such pleasure in how the hue changes on each flower as it matures – the intense colors when they first open, leading to muted but still beautiful tones over time. Through the rose, possibly more than with any other flower, God's awesome love extends, reveals, and touches us in greater intimacy with him.

God's Love for His Son

The Jackson-Perkins catalog describes their roses as stunning, striking, luscious, fragrant, elegant, graceful, dramatic, captivating, fabulous, vibrant, exceptional, long-lasting, delightful, and irresistible. These same words could be applied even more to Jesus.

The roses are the stunning centerpiece of the garden: the pink ones remind us of his softness and gentleness; the white ones bring to mind his purity and elegance; and the red roses remind us of his unfailing love for us. Our perfect rose, *"crucified in weakness"* (2 Corinthians 13:4), without spot or blemish, was jeered at, mocked, beaten, flogged, and tortured. He loves us that much.

He is also loved by his Father that much. Immediately after Jesus was baptized, a voice from heaven said, *"This is my dearly loved Son, who brings me great joy"* (Matthew 3:17). The same words were spoken at the Mount of Transfiguration where Peter, James, and John heard God's voice from a bright cloud: *"This is my dearly loved Son, who brings me great joy. Listen to him"* (Matthew 17:5). God spoke of his great love of Jesus, his Son. Here are some other verses to consider:

> *"The Father loves the Son and shows him everything he is doing"* (John 5:20).
>
> *"The Father loves me because I sacrifice my life so I may take it back again. No one can take my life from me. I sacrifice it voluntarily. For I have the authority to lay it down when I want to and also to take it up again. For this is what my Father has commanded"* (John 10:17,18).
>
> [Father,] *"you and I are one – as you are in me, Father, and I am in you. … you loved me even before the world began!"* (John 17:21,24).

Collectively, these verses assure us of the true and deeply intimate love relationship between God the Father and Christ the Son, even before the world began. The love relationship that was established between God and his people began as he created the world – the profound love between God and his Son began even before that.

Love is contagious – this love does not end with the Father / Son, for it includes us:

> [Father,] *"I have given them the glory you gave me, so they may be one as we are one. I am in them and you are in me. May they experience such perfect unity that the world will know that you sent me and that you love them as much as you love me"* (John 17:22,23).

Bob Sorge, in his marvelous book *"The Fire of God's Love,"* describes God's love:

> *The most sublime theme in all of Scripture is the love of God. There is nothing higher or nobler toward which we can direct our meditation. God's love is altogether wonderful, beyond our complete comprehension, and entirely inexhaustible in its scope and intensity.* [1]

Many of the attributes of the rose help remind us of these same attributes in Jesus. He is infectiously beautiful and his love is contagious beyond all measure. His love is profuse and his love is profound.

---

[1] Bob Sorge, *The Fire of God's Love* (Greenwood, Missouri: Oasis House, 2001), 9.

Russian Sage

I had wanted to grow the enamoring Russian sage for many years, but this is my first opportunity. With spires of lavender-blue sent out as sprays of tiny flowers, the sprays remind me of the presence of our Lord with his unfailing love, for he is the fountain of life.

Your unfailing love, O LORD, is as vast as the heavens;
your faithfulness reaches beyond the clouds.
For you are the fountain of life, the light by which we see
(Psalm 36:5,9).

Making Disciples

The long-lasting, lavender-blue Russian sage is loved by many gardeners, giving the appearance of an ornate fountain, spraying water this way and that. The fragrance and taste of this herb is stunningly pleasant – the silver-green foliage is a beautiful contrast to the delicate lavender-colored flowers. In the winter, the plant stems turn silver-gray for an additional season of color.

To some, however, the Russian sage is more of a nuisance plant, more similar to a weed than a flower. The matured flowers can produce many seeds that sprout throughout the garden. These volunteers can pop up in the most unpredictable places, sometimes where a plant is needed, but more often where it is not appropriate.

The bigger problem with the Russian sage is that it sends out long runners just below the ground surface. At the end of these runners, possibly two to four feet from the parent plant, new plants will suddenly emerge. Removing the volunteers and long runners has been an irritant to some gardeners, but it is also part of its beauty.

Whether a person loves the beauty of the Russian sage or is annoyed by its invasive nature, the key to remember is it is just trying to create children. Fathom that: a beautiful plant desires to create other beautiful plants in its own image.

Jesus said at the end of his ministry on earth:

"Go and make disciples of all the nations" (Matthew 28:19).

In essence, he was saying *"Go make spiritual children, ones that are like-minded in Christ."* Jesus envisioned discipleship to be a regular pattern of his Church: sharing his love, encouraging one another, revealing Biblical truths, moving in his grace and the power of the Holy Spirit. When Christ is the center of our lives, the natural by-product should be children that have matured spiritually and share in his love.

The Russian sage models good discipleship in that it attempts to create more Christ-like children. Other pretty flowers also model this discipleship, but so do weeds — just as the Lord's will is to develop disciples, the devil is also attempting to develop disciples. We should remember this: if we stop making disciples, the weeds will continue to grow. Christians, we have an inner beauty that others need, and the Lord has designated us to be the ones that show it. Our Lord's unfailing love, emanating like a beautiful fountain within us, is his method for making disciples.

A Garden of Love

Showy Primrose

I am encouraged with a sense of love and forgiveness as I leisurely stroll past the showy primrose. Hundreds upon hundreds of soft pink flowers fill the landscape, just inches above the ground level. The mass effect of these mid-summer beauties reveals gentleness even during the heat of the day. As autumn approaches, the flower heads begin to drop off and the small green leaves develop spots of brilliant blood red, a reminder of Christ's forgiveness for our sins.

Forgiveness

The showy primrose, with their mass effect of soft pink, are aptly named "showy." In late spring, the flowers become a carpet of delicate pink with a subtle yellow touch in the center. Slowly, the flowers fade with the heat of the summer, only to reveal brilliant dots of blood red leaves, as if an artist stroked each individual leaf. By the peak of autumn, the few flowers that are left are soft accents to each leaf's variegated red and green effect.

To some, the showy primrose is an irritating and aggressive plant, while to others it is simply beautiful. To those that find the showy primrose to be invasive, they overlook a feature found in only a few plants: they are very forgiving. Underneath these lovely short plants is a network of roots that, once established, is difficult to remove. Simply put, it can handle a great deal of abuse. Soil can be placed on top and mulch can be added, only to have seemingly no effect a month or two later. Individual plants may even be yanked up, but the plants respond with "I forgive you."

Notice the role of forgiveness in the following verses:

> *Since God chose you to be the holy people he loves, you must clothe yourselves with tenderhearted mercy, kindness, humility, gentleness, and patience. Make allowance for each other's faults, and forgive anyone who offends you. Remember, the Lord forgave you, so you must forgive others. Above all, clothe yourselves with love, which binds us all together in perfect harmony. And let the peace that comes from Christ rule in your hearts. For as members of one body you are called to live in peace. And always be thankful* (Colossians 3:12-15).

Our Lord is calling us to be people of grace and forgiveness. Kindness rather than bitterness is our place in Jesus Christ. We all get offended at one time or another – it seems that the further we go in our Christian walk, the more exposure we get to unkind actions. Sometimes it is our spouse, our children, our parents, or a close friend that we should be able to rely upon in love. Be assured that people will always disappoint us.

David Augsburger, in his classic book entitled *The New Freedom of Forgiveness*, states:

> *To forgive, to accept, to move again into right relationship, to be brothers and sisters again are not matter of words. They are deeds, acts, gestures of love, simple steps of acceptance – caring enough to feel the other's pain for a moment and then doing for the other what you would want done for you.* [2]

As the showy primrose, with its delicate pink flowers and red-tipped autumn leaves, is able to overcome the offense of the gardener, so should we be showing true forgiveness by restoring the relationship to the fullest extent possible and demonstrating it with acts of love.

---

[2] David Augsburger, *The New Freedom of Forgiveness* (Chicago: Moody Press, 2000), 117.

Index

Adversity – 21
Anemone – 2
Aroma – 47
Astilbe – 4
Autumn joy – 6
Bellflower – 8
Blanket flower – 10
Bleeding heart – 12
Cannons – 9
Chrysanthemum – 14
Children of the light – 11
Columbine – 16
Compassion – 13
Coneflower – 18
Controlled by the Holy Spirit – 43
Cosmos – 20
Cranesbill – 22
Crown of righteousness – 19
Daffodils – 24
Deep love – 31
Delphinium – 26
Depth of the love of Christ – 3
Discipleship – 59
Encouragement – 53
Endurance – 19
Faith – 51
Faith Chapel – iii
Flax – 28
Forget-me-not – 30
Forgiveness – 61
Fullness in Christ – 23
Garden phlox – 52
Gaura – 32
Gentleness – 5, 45
Gethsemane Prayer Garden – iii
God's love for his Son – 57
Good Samaritan – 39
Grace – 41
Grape hyacinth – 34
Hardy geranium – 23
Harmony – 29
Holy Spirit helps us love – 33
Holy Spirit's control over our minds – 43
Honeysuckle vine – 36
Humility – 5, 55
Hyacinth – 35

Hyssop – 38
Intimate love – 31
Iris – 40
Jacob's ladder – 42
Japanese anemone – 2
Joy in loving – 7
Kindness – 17
Lamb's ear – 44
Lavender – 46
Lily – 48
Love – the highest Goal – 9
Love gift from God – 27
Love in action – 39
Love of Christ – 3
Love our Lord – 31
Love your enemies – 21
Making disciples – 59
Marsh marigold – 50
Mercy – 39
Mum – 14
New journey with Christ – 25
Obedience to Christ – 35
Orchestra – 9
Patience – 19
Peace – 37
Perfume – 47
Perseverance – 19, 45
Phlox – 52
Pleasing fragrance – 47
Primrose – 54
Purple coneflower – 18
Reconciliation – 15
Rest for our souls – 5
Resurrection – 27
Rose – 56
Russian sage – 58
Ruwach – 33
Scrim – 43
Showy primrose – 60
Siberian iris – 40
Soapwort – 28
Succession planting – 13
Suffering – 19
Trumpet honeysuckle vine – 37
Trust the Lord – 49
Wand flower – 32

About the Author

I am an author, a gardener and a developer of computer software. I have been the caretaker of the Gethsemane Prayer Garden since 2004, having the primary responsibility for developing and maintaining this garden.

I began my landscaping career in 1971 as a foreman for a small landscaping company in Syracuse, NY, working under the direction of possibly the best landscaper in the area at the time. After several years, rather than continuing in this career, I pursued computer software development. My love for aesthetically pleasing plantings, however, never waned.

Working with computer technology is constantly challenging, requiring me to be on my toes from the moment I get to work until I leave. As I approach my retirement years, I see the Lord moving me away from that more difficult area and into a much softer and restful place. There is a peace that I experience (and I suspect most gardeners experience) that is far from our modern hectic world. Even though the seasons change, the rains come, and the morning's coolness transitions to a much warmer afternoon day, the aura of the garden is somehow very soft and gentle.

In addition to the work at the prayer garden, the Lord is moving me into a most unexpected arena: authoring and publishing books. Throughout my life, I have never had a good command of the English language. I look back at my first book, *Joshua's Spiritual Warfare,* with awe and amazement – while I remember the long hours of writing, I am frequently overwhelmed with what the Lord did in giving the words and insight that made this book into the success that it is. I tell my wife 'Boy that's good!' not in a bragging sense, but because of what the Holy Spirit revealed. Often I cannot remember preparing one part of the book or another.

With this book, *A Garden of Love*, I am again in awe at the words that often flowed from my fingers as I wrote from our mountaintop retreat. In a two week period, I read the entire New Testament and authored the first draft of the vast majority of this book. I worked hard during those two weeks but it was during that time that I was more at peace that I can ever remember. The Lord deeply and profoundly revealed his love and how he wants me to respond. As I sat down to write about each flower, I rarely had a predisposed idea of what to say or how I would say it – the Holy Spirit was once again at work. The Lord was teaching me about his true love.

If you are a believer in Jesus Christ as your Savior, I invite you to do the same – take a retreat and search for what is most important: *"faith expressing itself as love"* (Galatians 5:6).

This book, *A Garden of Love*, is my third book. All three books are available at www.Bible-Discernments.com by visiting the eStore.

Joshua's Spiritual Warfare
Understanding the Chiasms of Joshua

by Thomas B. Clarke

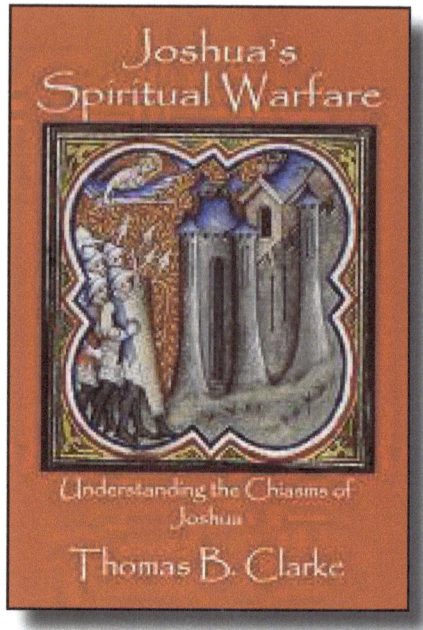

THE CHIASMS OF JOSHUA – A Profound Book for the Discerning

Theologians have been enthusiastically identifying chiasms in the Bible for over 200 years, noting that the center verses are normally the point of emphasis. While most seminary professors are familiar with chiasms, many pastors have not heard of it. To my knowledge, I may be the first from the Charismatic / Pentecostal perspective to do an extensive teaching on this topic. Using the Book of Joshua, this book adds to the understanding of chiasms by seeing the Scriptures come alive, uncovering many Biblical discernments, and applying them to spiritual principles for overcoming the enemy.

Enlightening

See Joshua is a new way. A **chiasm** (ky'-az-um) is a writing style that – once understood – clarifies, emphasizes, and reveals a deeper meaning in the Scriptures than is understood in just a surface reading of these same verses. You will see 67 chiasms that enlighten your understanding of the Book of Joshua; not an academic approach but presented so that God's messages are made more real and alive.

Revealing

This book is filled with revelation about the events in Joshua's life. There are analyses of chiasms, geography lessons, typological comparisons, and just plain good Bible discernment. As Rev. Barbara Di Gilio, Phoenix, AZ stated in her book review, *"It's only 232 pages, but it's packed full of good stuff, rare meat, just like I like it."* In this way, you will gain a whole new and more powerful understanding of Joshua.

Empowering

Please think about this regarding the life of Joshua: when the Israelite army went up against the nations in the Promised Land, was that in any way similar to spiritual warfare? [I hope you said Yes!] As you will see, the chiasms of Joshua show how to overcome the obstacles of the enemy. Each of the spiritual principles will lift you above defeat, empowering you to be an overcomer like Joshua.

The details in this book explain why chiasms appear in the Bible so frequently. If you are searching for a more profound understanding of the Scriptures, this book may be for you.

Copyright ©2008, Bible Discernments, 232 pages
Publishing Division of Prayer Gardeners

$14.99

A Topical Treasury of Proverbs

by Thomas B. Clarke

THE BOOK OF PROVERBS – A Comprehensive Compilation of Proverbs

Would you like to get more out of the Book of Proverbs? Do you desire to be a more virtuous woman or man? Do you want help with financial issues? Are you looking for hope? Are you searching for more wisdom? Now you can see all of the verses on any particular topic, easily organized for your full understanding.

Each verse of the Book of Proverbs is classified into one or more topics – there are one hundred topics. Based on the NET Bible, the words from each verse have not been altered. With this approach, we can stay with a topic, meditate on it, and let the Lord minister to us.

Organized

A Topical Treasury of Proverbs organizes the passages of Proverbs into 100 topics. No longer will you have to search through thirty-one chapters to find just the right verse or understanding for your situation. Every verse that is related to the topic is presented together.

Enabling

As you read through the topic or topics, allow the Lord to speak to you. By seeing each of these verses together, your mind will not be distracted with other unrelated topics. In this way, you can receive the full counsel of the Lord from Proverbs.

Time saving

This version of the Bible's Proverbs can be very helpful as a time saver. Concordances, even very good ones, do not go into this kind of topical detail. By putting the verses together with the topics, your research time will become much more efficient.

Effective

This 336-page book is printed with a larger and easier to read font, the same as what you are currently reading. **Emphasis** is added to each verse to show why the verse is categorized as it is. This means that the Bible verses become more effective in helping you understand how to apply them.

Copyright ©2008, Biblical Studies Press, 336 pages
Paperback $19.95
Hardcopy $29.95

www.ingramcontent.com/pod-product-compliance
Lightning Source LLC
Chambersburg PA
CBHW042025150426
43198CB00002B/68